THE BOOK OF CONTEMPLATION

The Forty Books of
The Revival of the Religious Sciences
(*Iḥyāʾ ʿulūm al-dīn*)

The Quarter of Worship

1 The Book of Knowledge
2 The Principles of the Creed
3 The Mysteries of Purification
4 The Mysteries of the Prayer
5 The Mysteries of Charity
6 The Mysteries of Fasting
7 The Mysteries of the Pilgrimage
8 The Etiquette of the Recitation of the Qurʾān
9 Invocations and Supplications
10 The Arrangement of the Litanies and the Exposition of the Night Vigil

The Quarter of Customs

11 The Proprieties of Eating
12 The Proprieties of Marriage
13 The Proprieties of Acquisition and Earning a Living
14 The Lawful and the Unlawful
15 The Proprieties of Friendship and Brotherhood
16 The Proprieties of Retreat
17 The Proprieties of Travel
18 The Proprieties of the Audition and Ecstasy
19 The Commanding of Right and the Forbidding of Wrong
20 Prophetic Ethics and the Courtesies of Living

The Quarter of Perils

21 The Exposition of the Wonders of the Heart
22 Training the Soul, Refining the Character, and Treating the Ailments of the Heart
23 Overcoming the Two Desires
24 The Bane of the Tongue
25 The Censure of Anger, Malice, and Envy
26 The Censure of This World
27 The Censure of Greed and the Love of Wealth
28 The Censure of Fame and Hypocritical Ostentation
29 The Censure of Pride and Vanity
30 The Censure of Deceit

The Quarter of Deliverance

31 On Repentance
32 On Patience and Thankfulness
33 On Fear and Hope
34 On Poverty and Abstinence
35 On Unity and Trust
36 On Love, Longing, Intimacy, and Contentment
37 On Intention, Sincerity, and Truthfulness
38 On Vigilance and Accounting
39 On Contemplation
40 On the Remembrance of Death and the Hereafter

THE BOOK OF CONTEMPLATION

Kitāb al-Tafakkur

Book 39 of

The Revival of the Religious Sciences

Iḥyāʾ ʿulūm al-dīn

بِسۡمِ ٱللَّهِ ٱلرَّحۡمَٰنِ ٱلرَّحِيمِ

AL-GHAZĀLĪ

Kitāb al-Tafakkur

THE BOOK OF CONTEMPLATION

Book 39 of the *Iḥyāʾ ʿulūm al-dīn*

THE REVIVAL OF THE RELIGIOUS SCIENCES

Translated *from the* Arabic
with an Introduction *and* Notes
by Muhammad Isa Waley

Fons Vitae
2021

Contemplation, Book 39 of
The Revival of the Religious Sciences, first published in 2021 by

Fons Vitae
49 Mockingbird Valley Drive
Louisville, KY 40207 USA

www.fonsvitae.com

The Fons Vitae Ghazali Series
Library of Congress Control Number: 2021939963
ISBN 978-1941610-558

Book design: Muhammad Hozien
Text typeface: Adobe Minion Pro 11/13.5
Editing and indexing: Neville Blakemore, Jr.

Cover art courtesy of the National Library of Egypt, Cairo.
Qurʾānic frontispiece to part 19. Written and illuminated by ʿAbd Allāh b.
Muḥammad al-Hamadānī for Sultan Ūljāytū Khudābanda, 713/1313.
Hamadan, Iran.

Printed in Canada

Contents

Many thanks to the Ihya circle: Zeb and Asghar Ali Shah, Asma and Azam Nizamuddin, Farah Abid and Fiaz Ahmed, Rasha Ali, and Haney Noureldin.

Preface

Of all the activities in which humans engage, none speaks more to our significance than thought. And all thought needs objects of thought, even if that means thinking about thinking. Meditation seems to be at the essence of many of the world's great religious traditions, and it usually lies at the heart of our spiritual teachings, the more esoteric side of the faith. To ponder is to consider, but no decision is implied: one merely reflects upon an object of thought. Meditation, best done in silence and solitude, demands a spiritual focus that enables us to have penetrating insights about the objects of our meditation. No one can do it for us – hence its importance in our individuality as a unique creation of the Divine: we are designed to arrive at knowledge of one's source, God. The Prophet Muḥammad, God's peace and blessings upon him, once came upon a group of people sitting in silence and asked what they were doing; they replied, "We are meditating." He then said, "Do not meditate upon God; rather, meditate upon God's creation, for you cannot bear to meditate upon God."

One of the words in Arabic for God's creation is *ʿālam*, which also means "world." The Arabic word derives from a pattern known as the noun of instrument. Hence, the very form of this Arabic word indicates that the world is used as an instrument to arrive at something else. Furthermore, the root letters of this word comprise the verb that means "to know." Thus, the world instrumentally enables us to know God, the manifestation of God's Attributes. Hence, to reflect upon God's creation properly will result in knowledge of its source. This is the root of metaphysics, the science of first principles.

There are many ways to ponder and reflect upon God's creation. Among the many matters related to meditation that this penultimate book of Imam al-Ghazālī's magnum opus, the *Iḥyāʾ ʿulūm al-dīn*, addresses, it teaches not only why and how one should meditate but, more importantly, provides the fruits of meditating, whether the fruit of intellection or inspiration. As the Arabs say, "It's not the rain we wait for but the fruits that spring forth from that rain."

It can be said that this extraordinary book explains the mysterious tenth book of Aristotle's famous *Nicomachean Ethics*, the purpose of our existence being mystical contemplation, an idea Aristotle left unexplored. The Qur'ān is replete with verses asking us to reflect, contemplate, meditate, and use our intellects, reminding us that essentially our highest purpose resides in doing so. Thus, it makes perfect sense that the Prophet, God's peace and blessings upon him, informed us that "One hour's meditation exceeds a year's devotion," (according to another recension, it exceeds devotion of sixty years).

This translation adds to the remarkable work of others who have contributed to Fons Vitae's wonderful efforts to bring the entire *Iḥyā' 'ulūm al-dīn* of the great imam to modern English readers. The seasoned translator, Muhammad Isa Waley, happens to be a practitioner of the path's practice. This book stands as a propaedeutic to the final chapter of the *Iḥyā'*, which is on death, the meditation upon which was a constant practice of our Prophet, God's peace and blessings upon him, who said, "Do much pondering upon the destroyer of delights: death."

Hamza Yusuf

بسم الله الرحمن الرحيم

Translator's Introduction

Ghazālī and his work

'Collect those scattered thoughts of yours,
 and you'll be filled with inner truths.
For God's servant, one moment's thought
 is better than sixty years' worship.
The mind's a falcon – thought, its wings -
 which soars as high as heaven's sphere.
Though its perch is the heart's tree-branch,
 it holds both worlds beneath its wings.
Now Earth's dustbowl is its carpet,
 now the Divine Throne's topmost bough.
Each moment it has some new task,
 all the time it hunts something new:
taking a mouthful of moonlight,
 then passing on beyond the sun…'[1]

THESE lines in praise of contemplation come from a poem by Ḥakīm Sanā'ī of Ghazni, a fellow-Khurāsānī Persian, fellow-sage, and younger contemporary of Imām Abū Ḥāmid al-Ghazālī. The text presented in this book is an annotated translation

1 Sanā'ī, *Fī al-fikr* (part), from *Sanā'ī-ābād*, in *Mathnawīhā-yi Ḥakīm Sanā'ī*, ed. M. T. Raḍawī (Tehran, 1348 *shamsī*/1969. For a full translation of this section of the poem see P.L. Wilson and N. Pourjavady, *The Drunken Universe: an anthology of Persian Sufi poetry*, pp. 45-47. The translation given here, and all other translations in this introduction, with one brief exception, are by the present writer.

of 'The Book of Contemplation' (*Kitāb al-Tafakkur*), the ninth of the ten Books comprising the fourth and final quarter of Ghazālī's masterpiece, *Iḥyā' 'ulūm al-dīn* ('The Revival of the Sciences of the Religion'). The title he gave to that quarter is *Rub' al-Munjiyyāt*, meaning 'The Quarter on Acts Conducive to Salvation'. The positioning of this treatise on *tafakkur* (translatable as 'contemplation', 'reflection' or 'meditation') immediately before the final Book of the *Iḥyā'* is noteworthy, for Book 40, 'On the Remembrance of Death and Its Aftermath', is climactic not only in its subject matter but also in its tone and effect – and was surely intended to be so. It is worth noting, however, that in Ghazālī's *Kīmiyā-yi sa'ādat* ('The Elixir of Eternal Felicity'), the Persian adaptation of the *Iḥyā'* composed for the author's Persian-speaking disciples towards the end of his life, *Kitāb-i Tafakkur* is placed seventh (as *Aṣl-i haftum*, 'Seventh Basis or Principle') in the fourth Quarter (*Rukn*), immediately after the Book on the related subject of 'Calling Oneself to Account and Self-Observation' (*Dar muḥāsaba wa dar murāqabat*), which by its nature requires reflection on and assessment of one's state and actions.[2] Consequently, the penultimate Book in the *Kīmiyā* is that 'On Love, Yearning, and Contentment [with God]' (*Dar maḥabbat wa shawq wa riḍā*), which is perhaps no less appropriate as precursor to the final, climactic Book, which enjoins and describes contemplation on the subject. Furthermore, in many other Books of the *Iḥyā'* the reader is invited to ponder the facts put forward in them and their implications and consequences.

There are several possible translations for the terms *fikr* or *tafakkur*, and for their Arabic partial synonyms such as *tadabbur* and *ta'ammul*. In this book, preference has been given to 'contemplation' but 'reflection', 'meditation', 'thinking', and 'pondering' have also been used. One reason for raising the subject at this point is that the question of terminology may have already have arisen in readers' minds. Another is that it provides an opportunity to cite, and to recommend, *Contemplation* - meaning the fine pioneering study of the subject in the context of Islamic thought and spirituality by the late Malik Badri. This book, the existence of which reduces

2 *Kīmiyā-yi sa'ādat*, ed. Ḥusayn Khadīw-jam, 2nd ed., vol. 2; *Dar Tafakkur*, pp. 503-526. *Dar muḥāsaba wa dar murāqabat*, pp. 483-502.

the need to expatiate at length in this introduction to what is a comparatively little-studied subject. It will therefore be referred to at various points in the pages which follow. Badri explains that he prefers 'contemplation' to 'meditation' because while the two terms appear to be generally synonymous, the second has been widely used in relation to spiritual practices in certain Eastern religions which are sometimes of a very different character from those he discusses. Badri adds that none of the words available in English convey the same spiritual resonance that the term *tafakkur* often does in Arabic.[3]

Contemplation as a healing practice

One author who researched and written about contemplation well before Imam Ghazālī's time was not (so far as is known) an adherent of Sufism but a polymath scholar who is by no means as well-known as he deserves to be, given the importance of his work; so Ghazālī cannot be faulted for not knowing about his work on contemplation, which was in any case carried out within the discipline of medicine. Abū Zayd al-Balkhī (d. 322/934) hailed from the region of Balkh in what is now northern Afghanistan but made his name, as did so many other men of learning, in the Islamic metropolis of Baghdad. Abū Zayd's treatise entitled *Maṣāliḥ al-abdān wa al-anfus* ('Treatments for the Body and Soul') is a masterpiece in two parts.[4] Of concern to us is the second part, dealing with the soul (though the first is also important), which is relatively brief but full of insights into human psychology. One of the author's main concerns is the remedial potential of directed thinking – what in today's terminology is called cognitive behaviour therapy. It is not

3 Malik Badri, *Contemplation* (London, 2000), p. xiv.

4 The only known manuscript of *Maṣāliḥ al-abdān wa al-anfus* is preserved at the Süleymaniye Library, Istanbul, as MS. Ayasofya 3741. It has been published in facsimile by the late Fuat Sezgin (Frankfurt, 1998), and its text in a critical edition with a study by Shaykh Maḥmūd Miṣrī, a Syrian doctor, *'ālim* and Sufi master (Cairo, 2005). In the latter book, the second part is found on pp. 505-564. The psychological section was translated with an introduction by the late Malik Badri as *Abū Zayd al-Balkhī's Sustenance of the Soul* (London and Herndon, VA, 2013).

possible to go into the full details, but one or two excerpts from al-Balkhī's treatise will at least illustrate where and how the practice of contemplation comes into the picture. Regarding the importance of the subject matter, Abū Zayd observes in his introduction that although there are people who are fortunate enough never to have need of treatment for the body, there are few who will never need treatment for the soul, for which reason nobody can afford not to pay attention to their psychological well-being. Putting forward a claim analogous to Ghazālī's, Abū Zayd concludes the preface to this section as follows.

'As for this type [of medicine], which is the treatment of the soul, we know of no one who has said anything extensive by way of exposition (*qawlan mashrūḥan wāfiyyan*) about it to the necessary extent. We shall therefore speak about it, to the extent of [our] knowledge]. And [all] success is through God.' Further on, he states that just as there are both external and internal means to preserve or regain bodily health, the same applies to that of the health of the soul; and that everyone needs to be aware of the limits of their resilience in dealing with adversity. As for preventive measures: 'One [means] is to guard oneself against outward factors, such as anything one might hear or see that could worry or disturb him by arousing anger, panic, sadness, or fear, and suchlike. Another [means] is to guard oneself against internal factors that would prompt one to think about any of the concerns that we have described which would cause the heart to be preoccupied and the mind to be beset with worries. There are only two ways of effecting this. Firstly, while in a peaceful state and with the soul's faculties at rest, one should make one's heart aware that this world was not created or arranged in such a way that anyone could acquire whatever they desire, or get whatever their appetites crave, without all of that [ever] being disturbed or vitiated by anxieties, preoccupations, or anything harmful or unpleasant occurring. One should grasp that this is in the nature and the normal way of things. One should not expect from this worldly life something that is contrary to its fundamental character.[5]

---

5 For an outline account of Abū Zayd al-Balkhī's work see Malik Badri, *Contemplation*, pp. 21-22, 104-106. For the psychological sections of his treatise, see *Maṣāliḥ*

In successive chapters Abū Zayd al-Balkhī discusses negative emotions and neuroses and their aetiology, symptoms, and relationship with physical imbalances and disorders. For each of these he describes means of counteracting and curing or ameliorating them through reflection and positive thinking: anxiety; anger; fear (*khawf*) and panic (*fazaʿ*); sadness (*ḥuzn*) and severe anxiety (*jazaʿ*), and satanic whispers (*wasāwis al-ṣadr*) and obsessions (*aḥādīth al-nafs*). The author believes that what lies at the heart of all neuroses and harmful emotions is anxiety, while its opposite, happiness and joy, is the root cause of all positive emotions.

Earlier Sufi masters on contemplation

In some of the early treatises on Sufism such as al-Kalābādhī's *Taʿarruf*, al-Sarrāj's *Lumaʿ*, and al-Hujwīrī's *Kashf al-Maḥjūb*, *fikr* and/or *tafakkur* is mentioned in passing, but none has a chapter on the subject. That certainly does not mean that contemplation did not play a significant role in Sufi practice from the earliest days of the discipline, and indeed in the spiritual life of the Blessed Prophet and his Companions; after all, it was in their time that *tafakkur* was enjoined by Divine Revelation in several Qur'ānic verses. Another noted Sufi author, Ibn Abī Dunyā (d. 281/894) is known to have composed a treatise entitled *Kitāb al-Tafakkur wa al-Iʿtibār* (The Book of Contemplation and Taking Note), but there are no signs of it having survived.[6] There are, however, two authors who manifestly influenced Ghazālī's thinking to a significant degree and whose notions of *tafakkur* are reflected in his work: al-Ḥārith al-Muḥāsibī[7], whose influence is openly acknowledged in Ghazālī's autobiographical work *al-Munqidh*

---

al-abdān wa al-anfus, ed. Miṣrī, pp. 505-564; and the (sometimes quite loose) translation in *Sustenance of the Soul*, tr. Badri, pp. 27-61.

6 Alfred Wiener, 'Die *Farağ baʿd al-Šidda* Litteratur', in *Islamica*, 4 (1913) p. 414; this article contains a list of Ibn Abī Dunyā's writings. His work is referred to as *Kitāb al-Tafakkur* by Murtaḍā al-Zabīdī in his commentary on the *Iḥyāʾ*, *Itḥāf al-sādat al-muttaqīn* (Cairo, 1311/1893-4), vol. 10, pp. 163, 164.

7 For al-Muḥāsibī's influence on al-Ghazālī see Margaret Smith, *An Early Mystic of Baghdad*, pp. 269-280.

min al-ḍalāl, and Abū Ṭālib al-Makkī.

In the teachings of the spiritual master from Baghdad we find much in common with those of Ghazālī where *tafakkur* is concerned. For al-Muḥāsibī this is one of the major 'works of the heart' and a practice of central importance in the spiritual path. It is an inward act of worship which lends strength to one's outward worship. Solitary contemplation contains the key to wisdom and is the means to progress from worship to the objective of salvation. Reflection has the potential to change a person's trend from disobedience of God to obedience, increase understanding of right and wrong, and induce love and glorification of God.[8] It is, in a sense, hard on the ego because reflection on the fleeting nature of this world and the everlasting nature of the Next eradicates from the heart the desire for worldly and selfish attractions. What makes it possible, and may eventually make it easy, is the acquisition of proficiency – with Divine help – in the concentration of one's thoughts, with the mind's passing thoughts cut off from disrupting one's *ḥuḍūr* (presence), and with presence of heart in contemplation of the desired subject. For al-Muḥāsibī, *dhikr* (a term which he often uses to mean *tadhakkur*, bringing to mind God and one's obligations to Him) is not merely connected with *fikr* (thought) but it is even a part of it. Such remembrance strengthens awareness that God, the All-Seeing, the All-Hearing, has complete knowledge of what is in the hearts of His servants; this leads to reflection, which in turn produces enduring certainty (*tathabbut*) as to what is right and wrong.[9]

Besides the benefits of growth in *taqwā*, or reverential awareness and fear of God, al-Muḥāsibī also advocates contemplation as a means of gaining knowledge. This strongly suggests the extent of his influence on Imam Ghazālī. Knowledge, says al-Muḥāsibī, is for the mind what a lamp is for the eyes. God granted knowledge to mankind in order that their power of reason might make use of it to realise (i) how the darkness of ignorance can bar them from recalling the Next World and (ii) that their Lord is constantly watching them. This leads us on to the related subjects of *murāqaba* and *muḥāsaba*, meaning respectively (i) constant vigilance over

---

8 Al-Muḥāsibī, *Kitāb al-Zuhd*; see Smith, ibid., p. 99.

9 Al-Muḥāsibī, *al-Ri'āya li-ḥuqūq Allāh*; see Smith, ibid., pp. 99-100.

oneself or ego and its behaviour and motivations and (ii) calling oneself to account at least once daily, scrutinising every word and deed. These measures are central features of the Baghdādī master's methodology of *mujāhada* (spiritual warfare or striving), thanks to which he acquired the *nisba* (associative name) al-Muḥāsibī; and by their very nature they entail habitual reflection. Together with *mu'ātaba* (self-reproach), *mushāraṭa* (setting rules for the *nafs*), and *mu'āqaba* (penalising it for breaking them), they form the main subject matter of Book 38 of Ghazālī's *Iḥyā'*, *Kitāb al-Murāqaba wa al-Muḥāsaba*, which immediately precedes *Kitāb al-Tafakkur*.[10]

Another feature of al-Muḥāsibī's methodology is the use of the imagination when contemplating death and its aftermath, chiefly as an encouragement to be God-fearing, forsake worldly preoccupations, and focus on preparing for the Resurrection, the Judgement and the Next Life. Remembrance of death is a frequent theme in his writings which may well have influenced Ghazālī. Especially striking is al-Muḥāsibī's evocation of the Last Hour and that which follows in his *Kitāb al-Tawahhum* ('The Book of Imagining to Oneself').[11]

Let us now move on to Abū Ṭālib al-Makkī's *Qūt al-qulūb* (Provision for Hearts), on which Ghazālī is known to have drawn extensively in the writing of his *Iḥyā'*. Abū Ṭālib has a great deal to say concerning *tafakkur* (contemplation) and *tadabbur* (pondering, a term used mostly in connection with reflection on Qur'ānic verses, or sometimes with Hadiths or other texts). Here it is only possible to touch on a handful of the many relevant passages from the *Qūt*. Al-Makkī advocates reflecting before one ever begins speaking (p. 150) or acting (p. 160); on one's own faults (p. 266); on a well-known Hadith that advocates comparing one's own state to that of those who are better off spiritually, and of those who are worse off materially (p. 490); on Divine bounties (p. 499); on one's misdeeds and the necessary conditions (*aḥkām*) for acceptance of repentance (*tawba*); and on everything that may happen to one,

10 *Iḥyā'* (Jeddah, 2011), vol. 9, pp. 117-224. Translated by Antony F. Shaker as *Al-Ghazālī on Vigilance & Self-Examination...Book XXXVIII of The Revival of the Religious Sciences...* (Cambridge, 2015).

11 *Kitāb al-Tawahhum* (Aleppo, n.d.), pp. 1-18. On this work and Sayyid Quṭb's commentary on the eschatological opening *āyāt* of Sūrat al-Takwīr (Qur'ān 81:1-14), see Badri, *Contemplation*, pp. 72-73 and 74-77 respectively.

to learn about the Divine wisdom behind it (p. 599).[12] In *Faṣl* 6, *Fī dhikr ʿamal al-murīd baʿd ṣalāt al-ghadā* (On the Disciple's Tasks after the Early Morning Prayer) – meaning between daybreak and sunrise - the author says:[13]

'This consists in engaging in recitation of the Qur'ān and in various types of invocation (*dhikr*) in the form of glorification (*tasbīḥ*), laudatory thanksgiving (*ḥamd*), and praise (*thanā'*; and of contemplation (*tafakkur*) of the immensity (*ʿaẓama*) of God (Transcendently Glorious and Exalted is He), His favours (*ālā'*), and the perpetual and simultaneous succession (*tawātur*) of His beneficence and Bounties – from where the servant [of God] expects and from where he could not expect, and that of which he knows and that of which he does not. One should [also] reflect on the deficiency of his gratitude for blessings manifest and hidden, as well as his incapacity to fulfil His command in respect of a high standard of obedience and continual thankfulness for the favour [He bestows]. Otherwise, he should reflect on the obligatory and recommended acts ahead of him [for him to perform]; or else on the dense veil of God, Blessed and Exalted is He; the subtle grace of His treatment of him (*ṣunʿih bih*) and His hidden kindness to him; the excessive lapses he has committed; and the past opportunities to perform righteous actions he has missed.

'Alternatively, he may reflect on the sovereignty of God Most High in the Sensory Domain (*Mulk*), His omnipotent power over the Spiritual Domain (*Malakūt*), and His Signs and His favours in both of them. Or again, he may ponder the punishments [threatened] by God, Mighty and Glorious is He, and the outward and inward calamities in them. Among [the Reminders of all] that are [God's] Words, Mighty and Glorious is He, '*And remind them of the Days of Allah*,'[14] which is said to refer to His bounties and is also said to refer to His chastisement.' Shaykh Abū Ṭālib then cites additional salient passages from the Qur'ān (7:69, 56:25, and 3:191). Next, he proceeds to contextualise the practice of *tafakkur*.

'There can be no beholding (*mushāhada*) [of the Unseen] except

12 *Qūt al-qulūb fī muʿāmalat al-Maḥbūb*. Ed. Saʿīd Nasīb Makārim. Beirut, 2010.

13 Ibid., pp. 21-22.

14 Qur'ān 14:5.

from [a basis of] certainty (*yaqīn*), certainty being the very soul of faith (*īmān*) and its increase and the specialised accomplishment (*fann*) of the believer. Some of the learned have said, interpreting the Tradition (*khabar*) "An hour's reflection is better than a year's worship", that it means the reflection which transports one from things that are displeasing [to God] to things that are dear [to Him], from appetite and greed to contentment and detachment. It has also been said that it means the reflection which causes the appearance of witnessing [spiritual realities] God-wariness (*taqwā*), and brings about remembrance [of God] and guidance.' The author quotes in this connection Qur'ān 2:63, 39:28, 2:219, and 5:89; he also cites Abū al-Dardā', one of the Companions of the Prophet, as saying that contemplation was his favourite form of worship. The remainder of this section enumerates further subjects for the discipline to work on, such as renewing his intention of sincere servitude to the Creator and service to Creation, and explains how to guard the heart against distractions. In conclusion, al-Makkī states that: 'These, then, were the acts of remembrance (*adhkār*) of the early [Muslims] and the acts of contemplation (*afkār*) of the [pious] predecessors. Remembrance and reflection were among the most excellent acts of worship of the avid worshippers (*'ābidūn*); and they are a short route to the Lord of the Universe...'

Contemplation also comes into the picture in Abū Ṭālib's instructions on acts of worship for the period before *zawāl* (the very start of the sun's decline from its zenith, which is when the time for *ẓuhr* prayer begins): 'The only *wird* (regular practice) in [that time] is recitation [of Qur'ān], *tasbīḥ* (glorifying God or, possibly, invocation using a *subḥa* or rosary), and contemplation (*tafakkur*); for this is one of the five times [of day] in which prayer was forbidden by God's Emissary (may God exalt and preserve him).'[15]

Contemplation is at least as much associated with night-time as with daytime; and in another section of *Qūt al-qulūb* it is mentioned in connection with night worship:

> 'And when arising at night [for worship], at whichever hour [the disciple] wakes up he should perform *wuḍū'* (ablution)

15 Ibid., p. 25.

> and perform [ritual] prayer or else sit down and recite [Qur'ān] or supplicate and perform remembrance of God…or else he should reflect upon His favours, His Immensity, and the inward aspects (*ma'ānī*) of His Omnipotence. Whichever of these he engages in, it is Remembrance (*dhikr*).'[16]

Further on, the author speaks about recitation at night:

> 'The people of night [worship] are on three levels: some of them weep when reciting contemplatively (*minhum idhā qara'a mutafakkiran bakā*).'[17]

Many of the passages about *tafakkur* in *Qūt al-qulūb* relate to Qur'ān reading, as do almost all those about *tadabbur*.[18]

Regarding the interpretation of the verse 'Thus does God expound His Signs to you, that you may reflect upon this world and the Hereafter,'[19] Abū Ṭālib comments:

> 'Even if one does not come near to that way of being so as to be, as [God] says, "*or lends an ear and is a witness*", [still] one hears from a place that us far off when to nearness and becomes one of the people of exposition and contemplation (*ahl al-bayān wa al-fikr*). As the Manifest Truth says, "*Thus does God expound His Signs to you, that you may reflect upon this world and the Hereafter*." That is to say, 'so that you may contemplate the evanescence and transience of this world and the everlastingness and perpetuity of the Hereafter; and give preference to that which is everlasting and perpetual, desiring it rather than that which is evanescent and transient and being detached from [the latter].' For with anything transient, its beginning resembles its ending, and its beginning is nothing; while anything perpetual is as if it never was less, and so its

16 Ibid., p. 52.

17 Ibid., p. 62.

18 Main references to *tafakkur* in *Qūt al-qulūb*, ed. Makārim: pp. 21, 22, 25, 62, 72, 119, 134, 149, 150, 160, 197, 208, 220, 266, 320, 375, 392, 411, 474, 490, 499, 568, 576, 577, 578, 599, 602, 677, 740, and 770 ; for *tadabbur*, see pp. 9, 27, 34, 54, 66, 72, 91, 82, 96, 124, 126, 127, 134, 137, 155, 179, 184, 186, 232, 246, 297, 313, 379, 380, 384, 404, 490, 505, 525, 535, 537, 538, 565, 577, 703.

19 Qur'ān 2:219-220.

> beginning resembles as its final state[20] in respect of being perpetual. Likewise, the All-Knowing, the All-Wise says: "*And the Hereafter shall be [infinitely] better and more lasting.*"[21] So He has described it, in respect of its perpetuity, using two adjectives which are among His own Attributes; as He says, Exalted is He, "*And God is [infinitely] better and more lasting,*"[22] and as He also says, Exalted is He, "*What is in your keeping ends, but what is in God's keeping is everlasting.*"'[23]

The remainder of this passage is interesting in terms of Qur'ānic interpretation. The main point, however, is that the above-mentioned train of thought – that (i) this world is transient, (ii) the Hereafter is everlasting, (iii) that which is lasting is preferable, and therefore (iv) the Hereafter is to be preferred – is one that Imam Ghazālī uses in his Book 39 as an example of *tafakkur* in a syllogistic form leading to a new knowledge or understanding (or, perhaps, 'reviving' or 'reinforcing' an existing one).[24]

Ghazālī's treatment of contemplation

Despite the masterly way in which Imam Ghazālī writes about *tafakkur*, and his immense stature in the Muslim world, there were later writers who were able to add to or comment on what he had said. Regrettably, it has not been feasible to survey the subject of *Tafakkur* in Islamic literature in detail as fully as it deserves, owing to the unavailability of so many sources (some of them very rare, in any case) at the time of writing. The coronavirus covid-19 (a wonder of creation in its own right, given its minute size and immense power to spread and to harm, disable or kill) is rampant all over the

---

20 The quotation marks are the translator's: this expression is a manner of speaking, since the word *ākhir* (in the sense of 'ending' or 'last part') cannot, strictly speaking, be used in connection with something that is everlasting.

21 Qur'ān 87:17.

22 Qur'ān 20:73.

23 Qur'ān 16:96.

24 The Book of Knowledge, Part 31 of *Qūt al-qulūb*, has been translated in full by John Renard: see his *Knowledge of God in Classical Sufism* (New York and Mahwah, NJ, 2004), pp. 112-263.

world, and in most parts libraries are closed. There being little of any prospect of them re-opening in the near future, it has seemed more realistic to work with whatever sources were available to hand rather than delay publication of the book. There are, however, a few important considerations that arise when assessing Ghazālī's work in the light of points raised by other authors. These will be discussed towards the end of this introduction. Now it is time to summarise the content of Book 39.

Imam Ghazālī's *Book of Contemplation* comprises four sections, preceded by an introduction. In the latter, Part 1, the author outlines the scope and purpose of the Book and emphasises the importance of reflecting not on the Essence or Person (*Dhāt*) of God but on His Actions and Attributes. In Part 2 he cites numerous sources showing the merits and benefits of contemplation, adducing as evidence verses from the Qur'ān, Hadiths (Prophetic Traditions), and sayings of renowned Sufis and of early Muslims (*al-salaf al-ṣāliḥ*) noted for their wisdom and piety. Ghazālī then proceeds to explain his own highly original views as to the true nature (*ḥaqīqa*) and fruits (*thamar*) of the practice of contemplation. Part 3 offers detailed guidance regarding the lines or avenues of discursive thought (*majārī al-fikr*) which are appropriate and productive. These fall into two categories. First come human traits and human actions, the latter being acts either of disobedience (*maʿṣiya*) or obedience (*ṭāʿa*) to God, and either obligatory (*farāʾiḍ*) or voluntary (*nawāfil*); as for the human traits, these are all conducive either to perdition (*muhlikāt*) or to salvation (*munjiyyāt*). The second category of lines of thought involves God Himself: firstly His Being (*Dhāt*), Attributes or Qualities (*Ṣifāt*), and Names (*Asmāʾ*), and secondly His Actions (*Afʿāl*), the latter being the most appropriate for human contemplation. In Part 4 Ghazālī explores in detail the various aspects of God's Creation, the 'Signs on the Horizons' alluded to in the Qur'ān, which when viewed with an observant, enquiring eye and considered with a worshipful heart are full of wonders and offer fertile, virtually inexhaustible, scope for human reflection. The author devotes especial attention to the marvels of the human body, but also considers the animal kingdom in general and the spider in particular; the earth and its mineral treasures; the creatures of the sea and its treasures; the creatures of the air, and phenomena of 'what lies between the Heavens and the Earth'; the skies and the celestial bodies; and the supernatural wonders of the angelic and higher realms of Creation. Ghazālī likens any human being who fails to look with awe and wonderment at the Divine handiwork manifested in our world and beyond it to an ant, dwelling in a tiny hole in a great and magnificent palace, which never takes the least interest in anything more than meeting its own daily needs. To fail to exercise our God-given ability to contemplate is to be guilty of negligence and gross ingratitude. To contemplate is, as we have seen, to gain knowledge; and although the extent of knowledge attainable by ordinary human beings is very limited, and even the most knowledgeable of Prophets or Angels know almost nothing in comparison with the Divine Knowledge, it is incumbent on every human being to seek knowledge in this and other ways; and the merits of contemplation is the point where this discussion began.

Contemplative methodology

The most notable difference between the treatment of *fikr* by Ghazālī and by most other authorities (with the exception noted above) is the prominence he gives to syllogistic thought: the juxtaposition of two observations, or given pieces of knowledge, and the logical deduction from them of a third. As we have seen, this process was described and advocated by Abū Ṭālib al-Makkī as one valuable mode of contemplation. In Ghazālī's *Kitāb al-Tafakkur*, however, his account of thought processes is almost entirely confined to reflection of this type. Moreover, Ghazālī frequently has recourse to syllogistic reasoning in arguments presented throughout his *Iḥyā' 'ulūm al-dīn*.

In connection with contemplation as a means to gaining knowledge, a key element in Ghazālī's spiritual methodology arises from the idea that knowledge transforms one's state, one's state informs one's words and actions, and these last in turn affect the state *(ḥāl)* of the heart, so that in a sincere person whose work (*'amal*) corresponds to his knowledge *('ilm)*, gaining beneficial knowledge will effectuate a 'virtuous circle' that can be summarised thus: CONTEMPLATION > KNOWLEDGE > STATE > ACTION > STATE.

The first two parts of this 'virtuous circle' are described in Book 39, with illustrative reference to the example he uses to illustrate the process of *tafakkur*: 'Before this knowledge [is attained], the state of the heart is love for the transitory life and inclination towards it. With the knowledge in question, the state of the heart changes and its will and desire are altered. Moreover, the change of will yields as its fruit such actions of the body as involve repudiation of worldly things and dedication to works performed with the Next Life in view.'

Imam Ghazālī also deals with the subject of thought and contemplation in many other parts of the *Iḥyā'*. This need not necessarily involve the syllogistic process described and advocated in *Kitāb al-Tafakkur*. An important mode of contemplation, which is not of course unique to Islam, let alone to Ghazālī, is to go over, explore, or rehearse something in the 'mind's eye', using memory and/or imagination. As he often reminds us, especially in Book 40 of the *Iḥyā'*, the believer should remember death and the Afterlife constantly, thinking of – or, we might say, visualising or imagining - the successive stages through which all must pass from the throes of death to the moment it arrives, then burial, being questioned and punished or rewarded in the grave, the life in the *Barzakh* or interworld, the Resurrection, the Mustering, the Traverse, the Balance, the Judgement, the moment of learning what is to be one's eternal destiny and destination (may God grant us all His mercy and forgiveness). As he puts it: 'If there is weakness in your faith, reinforce it by meditating on mankind's first formation; the second is similar, and is yet more straightforward. If your faith is strong, alert your heart to these terrors and hazards; and contemplate and reflect on them in detail.'

Contemplation also features prominently in Imam Ghazālī's treatment of Qur'ān recitation in Book 8 of the *Iḥyā'*. The author enumerates and expounds ten 'inward actions' in connection with reading the Scripture: (i) understanding God's speech and His bounty and kindness in revealing it to mankind; (ii) having veneration for the Divine Speaker; (iii) earnest attention and presence of heart; (iv) contemplating the meaning; (v) discernment, in the sense of reflection on specific matters in a verse, such as the attributes and actions of God or His Envoys; (vi) putting aside any potential obstacles to one's understanding; (vii) considering every verse as being addressed to oneself personally; (viii) receptiveness of heart, so that it feels fear, hope and so on in response to the content recited; (ix) ascension, meaning that one envisages (or, in the case of the spiritual elite, witnesses) oneself as being in the Presence of the Author Himself, Who is addressing Him; and (x) never being content or pleased with oneself, one's state, or one's recitation.

Besides those already mentioned, there is of course a vast range of other subjects that provide suitable 'food for thought': for example, one may think about the Creator and all He has given us, our parents and all they have done for us, and how fortunate one is to have some or all of the following: freedom, health, a family, a place to live, food to eat, a job, friends, and so on. Any of these may involve a syllogistic process but need not do so in order to be worthwhile or beneficial, for in them one may be, as it were, revising and reviewing knowledge rather than acquiring new knowledge as in the mode of *tafakkur* described in detail in Book 39. The recitation of Qur'ān should always be accompanied and complemented by pondering (*ta'ammul, tadabbur*) the meanings of the words one is reading. Furthermore, both here and in the practice of remembering death, the process may very well lead one to acquiring, without necessarily having tried or intended to, new insights, viewpoints or awareness; and these too are modalities of knowledge.

Contemplation in *Kīmiyā-yi sa'ādat*

Comparison between Ghazālī's treatment of the subject of contemplation in the *Iḥyā'* and the *Kīmiyā* shows the latter to be much more concise; in particular, the introductory section comprises just two sentences and six lines of text in the Persian edition, with a single Hadith. But another comparison is also called for, because Book 39 of the *Iḥyā'* and Book 37 of the *Kīmiyā* by no means represent the totality of Ghazālī's writing about contemplation. In addition to the material mentioned above there is more in some of the other

Books, especially in the *Munjiyyāt*. For example, in Book 1, *Kitāb al-ʿIlm* ('The Book of Knowledge') he includes among the traits of a scholar of religion who is truly oriented towards the Hereafter that 'most of his concern is with knowledge of the inward, watchfulness (*murāqaba*) over [his] heart; direct knowledge (*maʿrifa*) of the Way of the Hereafter and travelling it; and sincerely looking ahead with hope in the fulfilment of [all of] that... Wisdom that surpasses all bounds and reckoning is only accessed through striving and vigilance, proactiveness in outward and inward actions, and sitting with God Most High in seclusion, with presence of heart and in pure contemplation.'[25]

Furthermore, Ghazālī also left an Arabic treatise on the Divine Wisdom in Creation (*al-Ḥikma fī khalq makhlūqāt Allāh*), which describes more of the wonders of creation in nature, in some cases more extensively than in Book 39. The only text available to this writer was published in a compilation of Ghazālī's treatises: *Majmūʿat Rasāʾil al-Imām al-Ghazālī*. We shall return to this work later on.

It is interesting to compare passages of *Kīmiyā-yi saʿādat* with their equivalents in the *Iḥyāʾ*. Three examples will suffice to show that the difference is not confined to their length. Here is an extract from one of the key sections of the *Kīmiyā*, in which the author discusses the true nature of (discursive) reflection (*tafakkur*):

> 'The Reality of Discursive Reflection'
>
> 'Know that the meaning of reflection is the seeking of knowledge. All knowledge that is not self-evident needs to be sought; and that is not possible except by your collecting two cognitions (*maʿrifat*) and putting them together so that they may couple and from those two cognitions a third may be born, as a child is born from a male and a female. Those two cognitions are like the two sources (*aṣl*) of the third. One then combines them with the third in order that a fourth may appear from them. In this manner the reproduction (*tanāsul*) of pieces

25 *Iḥyāʾ ʿulūm al-Dīn* (Jeddah, 2011), vol. 1, p.264; cf. Kitāb al-ʿilm, *the Book of Knowledge: Book 1 of the* Iḥyāʾ ʿulūm al-dīn, *The Revival of the Religious Sciences*, tr. Kenneth Honerkamp (Louisville, KY, 2015), p. 210.

> of knowledge increases without end. If anyone is incapable of producing [knowledge] by this method, it is because he cannot find the way to those pieces of knowledge which are the [initial] sources. Such an individual is like someone who has no capital: how can he trade? And if he does have knowledge but does not know how to combine [two pieces], he is like someone who does have capital but does not know how to do business. To explain the true nature of [all] this is a lengthy matter. Let us [instead] draw a comparison. A person who wishes to know that the Hereafter is better than this world cannot do so until he knows two things about this world: firstly, that that which is everlasting is better than that which is transitory, and secondly that the Hereafter is everlasting and this world is transitory. Once he knows these two sources, this [third] piece of knowledge will of necessity be born from them: that the Hereafter is better than this world. We do not mean by this 'reproduction' what the Mu'tazilites mean; this [too] would require lengthy explanation. The true nature of all discursive though, then, is the seeking of knowledge by making two pieces of knowledge present in the heart. However, just as a sheep will not be born from the mating of two horses, whatever knowledge you may wish for will not be born from [just] any two [prior] pieces of knowledge. Rather, there are two specific sources for every type of knowledge; and until you make those two roots present in your heart this [specific desired] branch will not appear.' [26]

While the above passage as a whole echoes the equivalent part of the *Iḥyā'* as regards its basic message, there are one or two salient differences. For one thing, Imam Ghazālī goes further in his assertions about the means of gaining knowledge. The contention that 'All knowledge that is not self-evident needs to be sought; and that is not possible except by your collecting two cognitions' is more categorical than anything found in the Arabic equivalent. Taken literally, it seems to discount the value of any attempt to gain knowledge that does not involve discursive reasoning. So, for example, to

26 *Kīmiyā-yi sa'ādat*, ed. Ḥusayn Khadīw-jam, vol. 2, p. 894.

read a commentary on the Qur'ān and learn something about the meaning of a word, phrase, sentence, or allusion, would presumably count as benefiting from the commentator's insight and/or reasoning rather than one's own, and so it could not qualify as 'collecting two cognitions'. It seems more likely, then, that what Ghazālī really means is that *there are certain modes* of acquisition of knowledge which are only feasible in the manner he has laid down in such an exclusive manner.

In addition, there is an interesting difference between the *Iḥyā'* and *Kīmiyā* passages where presentational style is concerned. *Kīmiyā-yi sa'ādat* was composed, not very long before the author's death, for the benefit of those disciples in his own teaching circle in Ṭūs who did not understand sufficient Arabic to read the *Iḥyā'*. Here and there, this difference is reflected in the author's expository style and choice of language. In likening the process of juxtaposing two cognitions (*ma'rifat*) to the role of two parents in producing a child, Ghazālī came up with a metaphor that might have been deemed too 'earthy' for the more cultivated and urbane readership of the *Iḥyā'* – while it does have a partial counterpart in the English expression 'brainchild'. The same reproductive theme - this time with imagery from livestock breeding - is taken up near the end of the section, where the author adds an observation that is not found, as such, in the *Iḥyā'*: 'However, just as a sheep will not be born from the mating of two horses, whatever knowledge you may wish will not be born from [just] any two [prior] pieces of knowledge. Rather, there are two specific sources for every type of knowledge…'

In his discussion of the internal organs and other wonders of the body Ghazālī adds a few extra points that are not in the *Iḥyā'*, including another piece of homely imagery: the comparison of the stomach to a cooking-pot.

> 'More wondrous than all [other] wonders are those of the inner [parts of the body], the treasuries of the brain, and the powers of the senses that are placed within them. Indeed, the same applies to what lies within the chest and the stomach. For [God] created the stomach like a hot cooking-pot which is continually boiling so that food becomes cooked in it. The liver turns that food into blood and the veins convey that blood

> to the seven limbs; the gall-bladder takes the scum from the blood, which is like yellow bile; the spleen takes the dregs of that blood, which is black bile, from it; the kidney separates the water from it and sends it to the bladder. Similarly, there are [also, for example], the wonders of the womb and the organs associated with childbirth.'[27]

Our third and last sample passage from the *Kīmiyā* is selected to illustrate the manner in which Ghazālī adapted the text to his Persian audience by adding here and there some slightly poetic touches. There is also an explanation, not found in the *Iḥyā'*, of the Divine wisdom in the way in which the water essential for all living things is stored underground.

> 'Beneath hard rocks [God] has caused limpid (*laṭīf*) water to run, so that it may rise to the earth's surface, emerging gradually. Were it not held back by hard rock it would [all] emerge by a single route, and so the world would be drowned, or else [all the water] would reach the fields before they were able to absorb it gradually. Consider also the season of spring, reflecting on the fact that the surface of the earth is all dense soil; [but then] how when the rain falls upon it, it comes to life. It becomes like brocade in seven colours, or rather a thousand colours. Reflect on the plants that appear and, upon them, blossoms, flowers, each of a different hue and each lovelier than the last. Then reflect upon the trees and their fruits: the form and the beauty of each one, the scent of each one, the benefits of each one…'[28]

Ghazālī on 'The Wisdom in God's Creation'

Let us now turn to the other work by Ghazālī relating to this subject: the treatise referred to above, on 'The Wisdom in God's Creation' (*al-Ḥikma fī khalq makhlūqāt Allāh*). No English translation of this

27 *Kīmiyā-yi sa'ādat*, ed. Ḥusayn Khadīw-jam, p. 902.

28 Ibid., pp. 903-904.

treatise having been published,[29] this writer has taken the opportunity to present a summary. Adding five thousand words to this introduction may seem excessive to some readers, who are of course at liberty to skip the pages that follow. In favour of including this summary one might argue that in the first place, it is clear that Imam Ghazālī composed this treatise not to serve as a biology textbook but as an incitement to worshippers to marvel at God's creation and not to take it for granted. It is surely not without significance that a man who devoted his life to religious learning and teaching and to the spiritual path should have taken the time to investigate deeply the wonders of the physical world, about which only limited information was readily available in his time, and seen fit to cite so many aspects of it in detail and with eloquence.

In the second place, it is also the case that the wonders and beauties of creation are largely disregarded in our own time by many people, for all the tremendous wealth of written information and vivid visual testimony that is far more accessible today than ever before. Despite the Divine injunctions to contemplate 'the Signs of Allah', there are many Muslims who are ignorant and heedless of them. For these reasons, there is reason to hope that the Ḥujjat al-Islām (Proof of Islam) al-Ghazālī himself would not have objected to the inclusion of this material in a volume devoted essentially to his *Book of Contemplation*.

The verbal noun *khalq* in the title of the work, as with 'creation' in English, means both the act of creating and its product: that which is created, collectively and singly. Almost at the very beginning of his preface (*khuṭbat al-kitāb*) the subject of contemplation is introduced. Because of its eloquence it seems worth quoting the preface in full.[30]

> 'All praise is for God, Who has placed His bounty in the meadows of the souls (*janān*) of those brought near [to Him], has singled out for superiority among His servants the contemplative (*mutafakkirīn*), and has made contemplation of the objects of His handiwork (*maṣnū'āt*) a means to firmness of certainty in the hearts of those of His servants endowed

29 For a brief description of this treatise, with excerpts, see Badri, *Contemplation*, pp. 26-27, 94, 99-100.

30 *Majmū'at Rasā'il al-Imām al-Ghazālī*, p. 5.

> with insight (*mustabṣirīn*). They have found proofs of Him, infinite is He in His Perfection, in His handiwork. [Thus] they have come to know Him (*ʿalimūh*) and so have realized the truth (*taḥaqqaqū*) that there is no God but He and that He is One (*waḥḥadūh*). They have beheld His Immensity and Majesty, and so have realized His Transcendent Sublimity (*nazzahūh*). For He is the One Who is constantly upright in justice in every circumstance; and they are witnesses to that through observation (*naẓar*) and inductive proof (*istidlāl*). Hence they have come to know that He is the Forbearing, the All-Capable, the All-Knowing. As [God] has said in His Noble Scripture: 'Allah bears witness that there is no God but He, Ever Constant in Justice. No God is there but He, the Almighty, the All-Wise.'[31] And blessings and salutations be upon the Master of the Envoys, the Leader of the God-conscious, and the Intercessor for the Sinful, Muḥammad the Seal of the Prophets, and his Family and Companions, and [may] nobility and distinction [be theirs] until the Day of Judgement.'

In the introductory section of the treatise immediately following this preface we find a description of the nature and merits of contemplation that is at least as evocative and compelling as anything the author says in the *Iḥyā'* or *Kīmiyā*. Moreover, there are nuances in this passage of *al-Ḥikma fī makhlūqāt Allāh* which are not found at all in either of them and are too fine to be omitted from consideration here.

> 'Now to commence. My brother, may God grant you the success given to the gnostics (*ʿārifūn*) and combine for you the best of this world and of the religion [of the Afterlife]. The way to knowledge (*maʿrifa*) of, and reverence for, God (Incomparably Perfect is He) is through His creations, reflection upon the objects of His handiwork, and comprehending the wisdom in the various types of things He has brought into being (*mubtadaʿāt*), [all of] which is the means to firmness of certainty and, approaching the ranks of the godly (*muttaqīn*).

---

31 Qur'ān 3:18. The verse ends: '*The [true] religion in the sight of God is* al-Islām' (Islam, submission).

I have therefore produced (*waḍaʿt*) this book, alerting the minds of thinking people (*arbāb al-albāb*) to the definition (*taʿrīf*) of the forms of wisdom and blessings alluded to in a vast number of verses of the Book [of Allah]. For God Most High created the intellects and perfected their guidance by Revelation (*waḥy*) and commanded their owners to look upon His creations and to reflect upon and learn from the marvels that He has reposited in the objects of His handiwork. For He has said, Incomparably Perfect is He: *"Say, 'Observe what is there in the heavens and the earth'"*[32] and also *"And We created from water every living thing. Will they not believe?"*[33] There are also other clear, evidential and plainly expressed verses which anyone who contemplates them can understand. Those who advance in [grasping] their various meanings will gain immensely in knowledge of God, Incomparably Perfect is He, which is the means to [eternal] felicity and to winning the great good and increase which [God] has promised His servants. I have arranged [this work] in chapters, each describing the form of [Divine] wisdom inherent in the category of creation with which that chapter is concerned, in accordance with what has come to our minds in what we have [just] referred to. And this despite the fact that even if the whole of [God's] creatures were to come together to describe all that God (Infinitely Perfect and Exalted is He) has created, and the wisdom He has caused to reside in a single created thing, they would never be able to do so. That which they have been able to grasp of [all] that is what God (Incomparably Perfect is He) has granted to each of them and what has come their way, without even being asked for, from their Incomparably Perfect Lord. And it is God we ask that He bring us benefit by [this work], through His mercy and munificence.'[34]

After this introduction Ghazālī embarks on a sequence of chapters that survey the wonders of God's creation. Although he does not repeatedly speak about the phenomena as providing ample subjects

---

32 Qur'ān 10:101.

33 Qur'ān 21:30.

34 *Majmūʿat Rasāʾil al-Imām al-Ghazālī*, pp. 5-6.

for contemplation, as he does in *Kitāb al-Tafakkur*, he maintains a tone of wonderment which implicitly encourages it. Several of these have equivalents in the *Iḥyā'* and *Kīmiyā*, and while their contents overlap they are by no means the same. Three chapters are devoted to the elements water, air, and fire, and the wisdom in their creation, subjects not discussed as such in the Book of *Tafakkur* of either the *Iḥyā'* or the *Kīmiyā*. There is also a chapter concerning earth, but its subject is not earth as one of the four elements but the planet Earth, home and sustainer of terrestrial creation.

First comes a 'Chapter on Contemplating the Heavens and this World' (*Bāb al-Tafakkur fī khalq al-samā' wa fī hādhā al-'ālam*). Ghazālī compares the world to a house and describes and praises the colours and other beautiful aspects of nature and their effect on the beholder. Both people and other creatures derive comfort and delight from looking at the green of the earth and the blue of the sky, and guidance from the stars and the pathways they provide. In fact, the wise have listed ten spiritual, psychological and physical benefits of looking at the sky, which moreover is 'the *qibla* of those making supplication'. All of this, says the author, testifies to the perfect wisdom of its Creator.

The title of the second chapter, as given in the 'Ilmiyya and Tawfīqiyya editions, is 'the wisdom of the sun' (*Bāb Ḥikmat al-shams*), although it seems likely that the correct title (in keeping with the pattern of the subsequent chapter titles) is *Bāb Ḥikmat khalq al-shams* 'the wisdom in the creation of the sun'. Ghazālī asserts that only God knows the whole of the wisdom behind its creation; and he points out that but for its movements in relation to the Earth (as understood in his time) there would be no alternation of daytime with night-time and no year with its changing seasons, all of which would profoundly affect not only mankind but the animal and, to a yet greater extent, the vegetable kingdoms as well.

The third chapter is devoted to 'the wisdom in the creation of the moon and the stars' (*Bāb Ḥikmat khalq al-qamar wa al-kawākib*). These bodies, besides giving light at night, also serve to help travellers find their direction, and the author gives especial attention to navigation by the stars. Even more essential in his view, and according to ancient and mediaeval cosmology, are the stability and the regular rotation of the concentric spheres (*aflāk*) of the heavens, which are also crucial to the well-being of the Earth.

The fourth chapter concerns 'the wisdom in the creation of the Earth' (*Bāb Ḥikmat khalq al-arḍ*). God has made much of the Earth's surface soft, smooth and flat enough for mankind and other creatures to make their way around it with ease and to be able to rest. It is suitable for raising animals and growing crops, and is supplied with water to meet the needs of all living things. The dead can be buried beneath it, as can any harmful or unpleasant objects. From beneath its surface come both precious and useful minerals and metals, which are enumerated more fully than in Book 39 of the *Iḥyā'*. Ghazālī also touches on the variety of what we would call biomes and habitats, and the life and activities generated or enabled by them. Absent from *Kitāb al-Tafakkur* is Ghazālī's description of mountains (particularly their interiors) as vital stores of water; forests where great trees grow that are suitable for timber for buildings and ships; reference points for travellers on land and sea to get their bearings; and refuges and hiding-places for beleaguered or outnumbered groups or troops.

The fifth chapter is devoted to 'the wisdom in the creation of the Sea' (*Bāb Ḥikmat khalq al-baḥr*). This chapter's contents do largely mirror those of its counterpart in Book 39. To summarise: the Earth's seas are far vaster than its dry land; for every type of land creature a corresponding marine one exists; the sea produces pearls, corals and ambergris; it also yields fish wholesome to eat; water enables ships to float, and sea travel enables mankind to reach distant places unreachable by other means; and the winds and tides are made subservient to that purpose. Lastly, the physical properties of water, which we tend to take for granted, are an extraordinary, multifaceted aspect of Divine Wisdom.

It is surprising that this last point was not saved for the sixth chapter – the first of four concerned with the elements – which discusses 'the wisdom in the creation of Water' (*Bāb Ḥikmat khalq al-mā'*). Ghazālī reiterates its preciousness and its being taken for granted. He praises the qualities that delight drinkers, animal as well as human; wonders at how water reaches treetops and all parts of other plants, despite the force of gravity and ambient heat.

He then reminds us of its cleansing functions; how its moistness enables earth, clay and other substances to be shaped and made into artefacts; how it puts out fire; and its use in cooking for making hard or raw foodstuffs edible. In short, for a myriad reasons water is an inestimable blessing, essential to life on Earth. One might add that water is given a very prominent place in the Qur'ānic descriptions of Paradise, and indeed of Hell.

The seventh chapter concerns 'the wisdom in the creation of Air' (*Bāb Ḥikmat khalq al-hawā'*). According to the scientific understanding of our author's time, the world's creatures would perish without air, as the sea's creatures would without water, because air moderates the heat which would otherwise overcome them. Without the winds, rainclouds would not form and move, rain would fall heavily in separate, concentrated and hence ruinous torrents rather than in separate drops, noxious odours and causes of disease would linger undispersed, sea travel would be impossible, and crops would not be fertilised.

The eighth chapter is devoted to 'the wisdom in the creation of Fire' (*Bāb Ḥikmat khalq al-nār*). This element too is essential to human life. Because of its destructive potential, God has kept the fire which is latent in inflammable substances within them until they are kindled.[35] The benefits of fire include cooking, smelting, and working metal to make useful and/or decorative objects; and it provides humans with comforting warmth and light.

The ninth chapter, which is much the longest, explores 'the wisdom in the creation of humankind' (*Bāb Ḥikmat khalq al-insān*). Ghazālī first speaks of the miracle of human creation and reproduction and the development of the embryo. He covers nearly all the features to which he draws attention in Book 39, remarking on the combination of utility, beauty and wisdom inherent in every aspect. He starts with the face and head, including the teeth, then considers the outer senses, the vocal organs, the distinctiveness of every voice, the arms and hands, the legs and feet, all the bones and their structure, the skull, the spine, the muscles, and the internal organs. All these are wonders of Divine handiwork and are fashioned upon the basis of a single sperm-drop. Consider, then, says the author, the wonders

35 See Qur'ān 56:71-73.

of the heavens, whose creation is far mightier; and be aware that there is not an atom in all of the universe which does not contain evidences of Divine Wisdom.

Next, Ghazālī outlines the successive stages of physical and mental development of the human being, before and after birth, explaining the wisdom behind the slow and gradual nature of the process and focusing on particular features of this. Signs of Divine Wisdom include the differences between male and female, old and young, and so on, and the problems that would have arisen without them. This is one of the most thought-provoking sections of the treatise. Each part of the body, Ghazālī continues, is admirably suited to its function; some of the most wonderful functions are those of reproduction, digestion and nutrition and elimination, and those of the vocal organs. As for the outward senses, their value can perhaps best be gauged by imagining life without them and the deprivation and difficulties of those who are blind, deaf or dumb or mentally handicapped. Again, there is wisdom in our having, for example, one head rather than two, but also in our having two arms and two legs. Certain organs benefit from being located in parts of the body that are generally concealed. There are aesthetic as well as practical considerations in the placement of certain features, such as the hairs on the face – those common to both genders as well as those peculiar to males.

The body is like a household, with different people performing different functions within it; if a single one were missing the house would be in disorder. All the appetites, and all the emotions, implanted in man have a vital function. Another aspect of Divine wisdom essential to humans' wellbeing is their power to remember, and also to forget; without the latter one would be at risk of living in perpetual sadness. Three further blessings, among those differentiating us from other animals, are shame and modesty (*ḥayāʾ*), rational speech (*nuṭq*), and writing (*katāba*). (To the objection that the existence of different languages suggests that writing is a skill acquired by humans, Ghazālī's response is that the mental and physical processes involved in writing show it to be a Divine gift, and that the same applies analogously to speech.) Human emotions are also part of the Divine wisdom and each has a purpose, although they need to be moderated; those mentioned are anger, envy and hope. Finally, in an almost poetic passage the author extols the limitless variety of phenomena in our world (flavours, birdsong, riding-beasts, gems, and clothing, for example), the number and extent of which are known only to the All-Wise, the All-Knowing, Whose Mercy and Knowledge encompass all things.

In the tenth chapter, 'Conclusion to this Subject' (*khātima li-hādhā al-bāb*), Imam Ghazālī discourses on the rational intellect (*ʿaql*) as one of the greatest wonders and Divine benefactions to humankind. Through the intellect man can distinguish truth from falsehood; furthermore, an intellectual proof is more compelling than one gained through sense perception. Man is capable of realising that he is at one and the same time someone who is able to exercise his will and is active in bringing about causes and changes and creating things - and who is also passive and subject to change; he is not an independent and able to do whatever he wishes but is contingent and is part of created things. The human heart is the locus for the light that brings direct, unmediated knowledge (*maʿrifa*) of the Divine, and this is part of the 'ennobling of the Children of Adam' alluded to in Qur'ān 17:70. The heart and intellect receive guidance from Divine Revelation brought by the Prophets, God's Emissaries, together with corroboratory proofs. Humans may also receive portents of good news or warnings in dreams and visions. (In this connection we may note that the angels, like the jinn, are not discussed in this treatise as they are in Book 39.) People's eternal happiness depends upon whether they choose obedience or disobedience to their Infinitely Generous and Wise Creator.

The eleventh chapter, like the second, has a title in the printed edition which is suspect: *Fī ḥikmat al-tayr* (On the wisdom of birds) should perhaps include the word *khalq*, 'creation', with the wisdom thus attributed (*muḍāf*) to the wisdom rather than to the birds. In any case, Ghazālī here enumerates some of the special features of bird species that display the Divine Wisdom, such as the lightness of their bodies and the thickness of the skin on their legs which obviates the need for feathers to protect them from cold and heat, which would impede their wading or swimming; the long necks and beaks of long-legged birds, which enable them to catch their food; curved wingtips which aid flying; the way that each type of bird has a beak shaped exactly to suit its requirements, for digging, dismembering prey, and so on; the extraordinary precision of the design of feathers, the ease with which they repel dirt and water, being made with densely-packed, delicate fibres, and the lightness and strength of their hollow stems; the tail-feathers, which aid in flying straight or in steering; the digestive system, which renders teeth unnecessary; and the reproductive system, which produces eggs so that pregnancy does not prevent flight. When their mate is pregnant, a male brings material with which to build a nest to protect the eggs; this, says Ghazālī, is a matter of Divine inspiration. With doves and pigeons, the pair then take turns in protecting the eggs and keeping them warm. Small birds wander here and there to find their food, a little at a time; this is in keeping with their inability to fly carrying large or heavy items of food in their beaks. Large aquatic birds which feed on fish, by contrast, are able to fly while holding their prey; and all aquatic birds are able to swim and dive. Imam Ghazālī also discusses the nocturnal birds and their special features. He includes bats in this category, explaining that it is one of the signs of the Divine Omnipotence to have created furry creatures that can fly and fish that can fly. The majestic soaring flight, acute vision, and speed of raptor birds (*kawāsir*) are another wonder of God's creation in the animal kingdom.

Chapter Twelve continues the exploration of that kingdom, being entitled *Fī hikmat khalq al-bahā'im* (On the wisdom in the creation of animals). Imam Ghazālī begins by quoting Qur'ān 16:8: 'And horses, mules, and donkeys for you to ride and as things of beauty (*zīnatan*).' These quadrupeds are created with sufficient strength and sense to be of great benefit to humankind (including also carrying loads and turning mills), but are not too hard to sit on or too intelligent to be submissive to human control. They are an immense blessing, the author continues; and without them, we would (until the modern age of mechanisation) have struggled to achieve various tasks and never had time to cultivate the pursuit of knowledge or other activities peculiar to *homo sapiens*. As for predatory animals, they were created with the strength, speed, eyesight, sharp teeth, and other attributes necessary for hunting prey; they would represent a dire and continual threat to humans but for the Divinely appointed limits to their intelligence and, in many cases, their nocturnality.

Other beasts, too, are created with features appropriate to their mode of life; and their young naturally follow their mothers around and in most cases are very soon able to do so without being carried, unlike infant humans, and then to progress towards becoming independent; and baby chickens do so soon after hatching. Ghazālī points out the wisdom in creatures having either two or four legs, enabling them to walk around, and in their having one or two legs to stand firm while the other, or others, move; and he lists some of the benefits to mankind of the quadrupeds. The propensity of animals such as sheep to graze and move together is what enables them to be watched and herded by a single person.

Another animal possessing multiple benefits (even in the eyes of a great Muslim scholar) is the dog. Originally a predator, it has been tamed and is easy to train for the purposes of guarding and herding as well as hunting. By barking it is easily able to raise the alarm, and in its teeth and claws it possesses sharp and powerful weapons. Moreover, it is a loyal servant to its master and will even work without sleep or food when necessary. Indicative of the range of Imam Ghazālī's observations is a passage in which he points to the great wisdom in the genitals of female quadrupeds being located at the back of the animal to facilitate reproduction. Next he speaks of the fur and hair of animals which protects them from extremes of climate, and the various types of feet they have according to their needs. Human beings enjoy the immense blessing of having clothing and enjoying choice in what they wear. The author is impressed, too, by the manner in which many creatures find a hiding-place in which to die, so that one does not ordinarily see many dead animals; possibly he was unaware of the extent to which some creatures feed on the corpses of others. He also remarks on the functions of animals' whiskers and in particular their tails, and how they twitch their bodies to repel flies and suchlike if they land on a part which the head and tail cannot reach. Other wonders of animal creation to be wondered at are the elephant's trunk, the giraffe's neck, and the fox's cunning. From humanity's point of view, Divine Wisdom having made the animals diverse by nature is a manifold blessing. Those which we eat feed on plants, those which carry burdens are placid, those which are fierce but are of use to us (elephants and cats included) can be tamed and in some cases trained, as can birds both placid (pigeons and doves) and fierce (falcons).

Ghazālī concludes this chapter by remarking that what is unknown about the Divine Wisdom in respect of the animal kingdom far exceeds that which is known.

The thirteen chapter takes us down to the level of smaller creatures, being headed *Fī ḥikmat khalq al-naḥl wa al-naml wa al-ʿankabūt wa dūd al-qazz wa al-dhabāb wa ghayr dhālik* ('On the wisdom in the creation of bees, ants, spiders, silkworms, flies, etc.') Imam Ghazālī begins by describing how ants collaborate in gathering and storing food, and in the construction of their underground homes safe from extremes of weather and from flooding.[36] As for bees, their wondrous aspects include having a single queen (which the author calls the *ra'īs*, 'head', and refers to as male) to each hive, the construction of their homes from hexagonal cells, the collection of pollen and nectar from which they produce honey, and the making of beeswax which is also of benefit to humans, especially - but not only - for candles. Next, the skill and ingenuity of the spider are described in terms broadly similar to Book 39.

Not mentioned in that Book is the silkworm (actually a caterpillar or larva), singled out here by the author as having been created purely for the benefit of human beings. Ghazālī describes how the silkworm lives and feeds on mulberry leaves and then, after its silk-spinning career is over, dies (or, rather, appears to), and is then resurrected in the form of a moth, which is the form in which this species reproduces. (Our author might have been interested to know that an average cocoon contains one thousand yards of silk thread, but horrified to learn that in modern times this fabricator of shimmering beauty is very often rewarded, on its retirement, by being killed with an infusion of hot air or steam.) From the fruits

36 For the wonders of the ant see also Badri, *Contemplation*, p. 95-97, who quotes Imam and Caliph ʿAlī ibn Abī Ṭālib (in al-Sharīf al-Raḍī, *Nahj al-balāgha*, tr. Sayed Ali Reza, pp. 370-371), Ibn al-Qayyim al-Jawziyya (*Miftāḥ al-saʿāda*, vol. 1, pp. 242-243), and a modern Egyptian author, Muṣṭafā Maḥmūd (*Lughz al-hayāh*, pp. 47-49).

of this tiny creature's labour humankind make garments of great beauty. Other wonders of creation are the monitor lizard (*sibaʿ al-ḍabāb*), with its exceptional eyesight and speed of flight from a still position; and the scorpion, with its hunting technique of pouncing on its prey from above. The accomplishments of the crow or raven, and of birds of prey, also receive passing mention. Next comes the chameleon, master of camouflage; Ghazālī provides a vivid picture of the way it conceals itself and then shoots out its long, sticky tongue, 'about three handspans in length', 'at lightning speed' (in a time recorded at 0.007 seconds) to catch its prey. Finally there is the mosquito, which has the gift of tracing with ease where to find the blood on which it feeds. This tiny insect is so astounding that if all the inhabitants of the heavens and the Earth banded together to create such a thing they would not be able to.

Chapter Fourteen has a long-winded title: 'On the wisdom of, and manifestations of wisdom contained in, the creation of fish' (*Fī hikmat khalq al-samak wa mā taḍamman khalquhā min al-ḥikam*). In fact, however, it discusses aquatic creatures of various kinds, beginning with fish, of which there are innumerable varieties. What they have in common are fins and tailfins, which the author calls 'wings' and 'tails', instead of legs, perfectly suited to propulsion and steering underwater; skins that are light but resilient; and the sense of sight, hearing, and smell. Some of them are food for others, and some for humans and birds. Accordingly, they have been created to reproduce in great number, with females generally producing large clusters of eggs while some species have characteristics of both genders and are parthenogenetic. Then there are creatures (not fish but reptiles) such as turtles and crocodiles, which have fore and hind legs; these (according to Ghazālī, who in this instance was ill-informed)) lay single eggs which hatch by themselves in the heat, and the hatchlings which then emerge need no help, thanks to the Divine wisdom, in finding and consuming food or in meeting their other needs. Those fish which are predators are provided with hard, thick skins and plenty of razor-sharp teeth.

By contrast, there are sea creatures, such as varieties of shellfish and snails, which are soft, vulnerable and immobile (or almost so) but are protected by thick, hard shells and in some cases can attach themselves inextricably to rocks or other hard surfaces. Starfish are able to retract their heads when their safety requires it and 'close the door' on their bodies in such a way that it becomes hidden. Another type of fish (Ghazālī must have in mind the squid and/or cuttlefish, which are in fact cephalopod molluscs) finds its food in the depths close to the shore; when threatened it releases ink from a sac in its belly which blocks the vision of its attacker and enables it to escape. There are fish that have wings 'resembling those of a bat,' which they use to fly from place to place over the surface of the water and appear to the uninformed to be a type of bird. Another type of fish, found mainly in rivers, avoids being caught by numbing the hand of anyone who touches it (this sounds like an electric fish, such as the electric catfish found in the Nile). In similar ways, God has provided for all aquatic creatures an appropriate form, characteristics, and means of finding provision, guiding each to its appointed way of life. Their wonders could fill volumes without ever being fully enumerated.

Chapter Fifteen is devoted to the wisdom and the wonders in the creation of plants and trees (*Fī ḥikmat khalq al-nabāt wa mā fīh min 'ajā'ib ḥikmat Allāh ta'ālā*). Imam Ghazālī starts by quoting Qur'ān 27:60, and then invites the reader to consider how the plants of the Earth beautify and adorn it, the Earth is like a mother to them, and the Creator has placed in them countless benefits to mankind, such as food items, scent, and colour. Seeds and kernels provide the protective environment for their initial growth, with certain ones having thick and hard shells to prevent birds from taking and eating them, God having given preference to humans in this form of provision. Harvested crops and fruit feed mankind, animals and birds. Trees supply timber, fuel, and many other things as well as fruits. Thanks to the *baraka* (power of blessing) imparted by God, from a single grain there grow a hundred or more. Thanks to His wisdom, mankind may use some of the grains they harvest for food and store some for sowing; the same applies to fruit that grows on trees. Among the miracles of Divine creativity are the structure and function of leaves, and the manner in which roots grow and absorb moisture and nutrients, all mentioned in Book 39. (Modern research shows that trees can communicate information to one another about their environment.[37]) The sprouting of leaves before fruit protects the latter from harm, and the spaces between the leaves, says the author, allow 'particles' of sunshine and air which the fruit needs to enter.

Another sign of God's mercy and creativity is the multiplicity of size, shape, hue, shade, smell, and tastes manifested in the plant kingdom (to which one might add the different times of year or season in which they fruit and/or flower). There are countless benefits in plants for humankind by way of medicinal and nutritional value, a theme which is alluded to in verses of the Qur'ān and expounded in *Kitāb al-Tafakkur*. The author then describes the remarkable features of date-palms, pomegranate plants and their fruit, and the way that pumpkins, melons, squashes and suchlike grow on the ground. All these wonderful aspects of Creation, says Imam Ghazālī, offer ample scope for those given to contemplation.

The sixteenth and final chapter is headed *Bāb mā tastashʿar bih al-qulūb min al-ʿaẓama li-ʿAllām al-Ghuyūb* (Hearts' realisation of the Immensity of the Knower of All Unseen Things). The author begins by quoting Qur'ānic verses, 17:44, 42:5, and 13:13, before summarising the main themes of the treatise.

Contemplation in Ghazālī's *al-Maqṣad al-asnā*

Another of Imam Ghazālī's works which is of relevance to our topic is his commentary on the meaning of the Divine Names, al-*Maqṣad al-asnā fī sharḥ Asmā' Allāh al-Ḥusnā*. Broaching the question of how and to what extent it is possible for a human to gain knowledge (*maʿrifa*) of God, he asserts that the utmost knowledge one can reach is the knowledge that in His Essence He is unknowable. At the same time, he says that although only God has complete knowledge of Himself, an *ʿārif* may gain direct cognition (*maʿrifa*) of Him through 'evidential unveiling' (*inkishāfan burhāniyyan*). Otherwise – and this

37 See e.g. Peter Wohlleben, *The Secret Life of Trees: a visual celebration of a magnificent world* (Vancouver, BC and Berkeley, CA, 2018). Also of interest is the same author's *The Secret Wisdom of Nature: trees, animals, and the extraordinary balance of all living things: stories from science and observation* (Vancouver and Berkeley, 2019).

takes us to the subject matter of *al-Maqṣad al-Asnā* – knowledge of Him in the form of learning about His Names and Attributes is accessible to ordinary people (*maftūḥ lil-khalq*). In that respect as in others, they differ in rank:

'Someone who knows Him to be Knowing and Powerful (*'Ālim Qādir*), Mighty and Majestic is He, is not like someone who beholds the wonders of His Signs in the Realm of the Heavens and the Earth and in the creation of spirits and bodies and becomes aware of the marvels of [His] dominion and the prodigies of [His] creative power, examining it in detail, realising to the full the fine points of [His] wisdom, doing full justice to the subtle aspects of [His] planning; and [at the same time] acquiring [himself] all the angelic qualities which bring one close to God, Mighty and Majestic is He, and attaining to the acquisition of those qualities [to the maximum degree possible]. No! Between those two is an immense gulf, one that can hardly be measured. And in respect of the detail and amount known to them there is [also] a disparity between [different] Prophets and Saints (*awliyā'*).' Ghazālī goes on to explain that it is also impossible for humans to have complete knowledge of the Divine Attributes, and the wonders and wisdom of God's creation and lordship of the universe; and that God alone possesses full knowledge of them.[38] For Ghazālī, as we have seen, to acquire *ma'rifa* of God's creation means not simply acquiring information but also contemplation: pondering it (*ta'ammul*) and drawing lessons from it (*i'tibār*). He contends that although the amount of knowledge that humans can acquire is limited, it is still virtually endless. To gaining a profound understanding of the Attributes of God, and to acquire as much of those traits as is humanly possible, is the goal which Imam Ghazālī has in mind in *al-Maqṣad al-Asnā*, the title of which means 'The Loftiest Objective'. It is also one of the themes and objectives which inform his *Kitāb al-Tafakkur*. Lest one lose sight of another side of the subject, let us remember that contemplating God's Attributes, especially (but not only) those of *Jamāl* or Beauty, is also a means to increase in love of Him.

38 *al-Maqṣad al-asnā fi sharḥ Asmā' Allāh al-Ḥusnā*, ed. and English introduction Faḍluh Shiḥāda (Beirut, 1971), pp. 54-55; cf. *The Ninety-Nine Beautiful Names of God*, tr. D. B. Burrell and N. Daher (Cambridge, 1999), pp. 42-43.

After al-Ghazālī

We have already heard from one of Ghazālī's Persian contemporaries, Ḥakīm Sanā'ī. In the following centuries there were to be many authors who wrote about contemplation and/or wrote works designed to induce it. Not all of them, of course, did so as a result of Ghazālī's direct influence. Authors who made important contributions in Persian in the 5th/11th to 7th/13th centuries include 'Abd Allāh Anṣārī, Farīd al-Dīn 'Aṭṭār, Aḥmad Ghazālī (brother of our author), Aḥmad-i Jām, Rashīd al-Dīn Maybudī, Najm al-Dīn Rāzī, Jalāl al-Dīn Rūmī, Maḥmūd Shabistarī, and Bahā' al-Dīn Walad. Out of all these riches and more, a brief fleeting mention of three examples must suffice. Anṣārī in his classification of the stages of the Path, describes *shuhūd* (witnessing) in terms resembling the concept of *fikr*; the *Ma'ārif* (Cognitions) of Bahā' al-Dīn Walad, Rūmī's father, are full of mystical reflections, many of them startling; and 'Aṭṭār, in one of his *mathnawī* allegories of the Sufi Path, *Muṣībat-nāma* ('Book of Trials'), makes Fikrat-i Sālik (Wayfaring Contemplation) the central figure, representing the human soul journeying through the material and spiritual worlds in its quest for ultimate Truth.

In the Arab world, one of the eminent later authorities who wrote on *tafakkur* was 'Abd Allāh ibn 'Alawī al-Ḥaddād (d. 1132/1720), who like all of the Bā 'Alawī Sayyids of Ḥaḍramawt in Yemen held *Iḥyā' 'ulūm al-dīn* to be the indispensable text for instruction in the Islamic sciences and for ordinary believers seeking to improve their spiritual life and moral character. Imam al-Ḥaddād's work *Risālat al-Mu'āwana*, translated by Mostafa Badawi as *The Book of Assistance* (London, 1989 etc.), presents in concise form a wealth of guidance on worship and ethical living. The ninth chapter[39] (*Book of Assistance*, pp. 31-35) is devoted to contemplation. It provides an excellent example of the ways in which later masters have adopted and presented aspects of Ghazālī's work, in this case assigning to it a central role in spiritual discipline. Imam al-Ḥaddād begins as follows:

---

39 *Risālat al-Mu'āwana*, pp. 55-61; *Book of Assistance*, pp. 31-35.

> 'You should have a *wird* of contemplation in every twenty-four hours, for which you should set aside one hour or more. The best time for contemplation is one in which there are the fewest preoccupations and concerns and the most potential for presence of heart, such as the depths of the night. Know that the state of one's religious and worldly affairs depends on the soundness of one's reflection. Anyone who has a share of it possesses an abundant share of all goodness. It has been said that an hour of contemplation is better than a year of worship. Said 'Alī, may God ennoble his countenance, "There is no act of worship like contemplation." Said one of the *'ārifūn* (knowers of God), "Contemplation is the heart's lamp; if it departs, the heart has no light."'

Imām al-Ḥaddād continues:

> 'There are many modes of contemplation. One, the noblest of them, is to reflect on the wonders of God's astounding creation, the inward and outward signs of His Omnipotence, and the signs He has distributed around the Domain of the Earth and the Heavens. This kind of reflection increases knowledge of God's Essence, Attributes, and Names. He has enjoined it, saying "*Say: Look upon what there is in the Heavens and the Earth.*" Reflect on the wondrous creatures He has made, and on yourself. He has said, "*In the Earth are signs for those possessing certainty – and in yourselves; can you not see?*" Know that you should reflect on the favours and bounties of God, which He has made available to you.'

The author then cites Qur'ān 7:69, 45:18, and 46:53, adding that 'This kind of contemplation results in the heart being filled with love of God and with continual thankfulness to Him, both inwardly and outwardly, in a manner pleasing and satisfying to Him.' The next theme for contemplation is to 'reflect on God's total awareness of you, and His seeing and knowing all about you,' in which connection the author cites Qur'ān 50:16, 57:14, and 58:7. The benefit of this is that one should then be ashamed to be seen by God in the wrong place, doing wrong things, or failing to do the right things. One should ponder on Qur'ān 51:56, 23:115, and 84:16, which 'will increase your fear of God and prompt you to accuse and rebuke yourself, avoid remissness, and persist in your [pious] ardour.' After that, says the author, 'You must reflect on this worldly life, its multiple preoccupations and dangers, and the rapidity with which it perishes; and on the Afterlife, its felicity and its eternal duration.' Qur'ānic verses cited as bearing on this theme include 2:220, 87:17, and 29:64. Such reflection 'results in losing all appetite for this world, and in strong attraction to the Afterlife.'

The next theme is 'the imminence of death and the regret and remorse that arise when it is too late', and the verses cited are 62:8, 23:99, and 63:9-11. The benefit of reflecting on them is that 'hopes become short, behaviour improves, and provision [of good actions] is gathered for the Promised Day [of Judgement].' Lastly, says Imam al-Ḥaddād, 'You should reflect on those attributes and actions which God has described His friends and His enemies as having, and on both the short-term and the ultimate recompense He has in store for each category.' The corresponding Qur'ānic verses for contemplation are 82:13-14, 32:18, 42:5-7, 8:2-4, 24:55, 39:40, 9:67-68, 9:71-72, and 10:7-10. The outcome of this is 'that you come to love those who are fortunate [in the Hereafter] and make a habit of emulating their actions and assuming their attributes; and detest those who are condemned to misery [in the Next World] and make a habit of avoiding their actions and their traits.'

The Imam concludes this 'mini-treatise' on *tafakkur* by warning of the dangers of trying to meditate upon the Divine Essence and Attributes with the aim of understanding Them with the mind. Before doing so he explains that there is far more to be said on the subject of contemplation: 'Were we to permit ourselves to pursue the various directions for reflection we would have to abandon the brevity we intended. What we have mentioned should be sufficient for people of reasoning. With each type of reflection, you should bring to mind verses, Hadiths, and narratives relating to it...'[40]

Modern psychologists have studied and researched thought and contemplation. Malik Badri's work has shown that some of their findings were known to Muslim sages many centuries ago. For example, thought-impulses (in Arabic *khāṭir*, pl. *khawāṭir*), known to modern

40 *Risālat al-Mu'āwana*, pp. 55-61; *Book of Assistance*, pp. 31-35.

psychologists as 'automatic thoughts' (and claimed by one of them as his own discovery[41]), were analysed, categorised and described in the 6th/12th and 7th/13th centuries by Sufi masters such as Shihāb al-Dīn Suhrawardī, Najm al-Dīn Kubrā, and Najm al-Dīn Rāzī. As for the modalities of contemplation, one modern expert who has produced new insights is Professor Badri himself. In *Contemplation* he proposes a fourfold categorisation: 'Islamic contemplation passes through three interconnected stages, leading to the fourth and final stage which I call the stage of "spiritual cognition" (*shuhūd*). The first stage is when [mental] knowledge of the contemplated object comes through direct sensory perception...or indirectly, as in the case of imagination...' The second stage involves closer examination and appreciation of that which is perceived, and in some cases admiration or even wonder. In the third stage, the contemplator is 'carried away', wholly absorbed in submission to the Creator of that which is contemplated. They come to realise that its Creator, the Maker of all things, is the One Unique Existent; there is none other. When such cognitions become established and reinforced with remembrance of God, the spiritual sensations and experiences become part of the worshipper's very nature. This awestruck mode of contemplation is what Badri means by the term *shuhūd*. He relates it to a saying of the great ascetic and Sufi sage al-Ḥasan al-Baṣrī, as quoted by Ibn al-Qayyim al-Jawziyya, a renowned 8th/14th century non-Sufi scholar who wrote on contemplation and much else: 'Men of knowledge have resorted to thought together with the remembrance of God, imploring their hearts to speak until the hearts responded with wisdom.'[42] One might perhaps add that this concept of *shuhūd* brings to mind the Qur'ānic verse '*We shall show them Our Signs upon the horizons and within [their] souls, until it is clear to them that it is the Truth. Is it not enough that your Lord is Witness over all things?*'[43] Those who attain the highest stage of *shuhūd* are also described in the chapter on *mushāhada* (witnessing [of inner realities]) in *Kitāb al-Luma'*, where the author quotes 'Amr ibn 'Uthmān al-Makkī as

---

41 Aaron Beck, *Cognitive Therapy and the Emotional Disorders* (New York, 1976), pp. 29-35.

42 *Contemplation*, pp. 30-31. Al-Ḥasan al-Baṣrī is quoted from Ibn al-Qayyim al-Jawziyya, *Miftāḥ al-sa'āda* (Riyadh, n.d.), p. 180.

43 Qur'ān 41:52-53.

stating in his *Kitāb al-Mushāhada* that such people behold God in all things and all things through Him, so that they are both absent when present and present when absent, seeing God as One and Unique in both cases, seeing Him as the Outward Who is Inward and the Inward Who is Outward, the Last in His Firstness, the First in His Lastness.[44] Badri cites another description, by Ibn al-Qayyim himself, of the level at which the seeker sees and hears nothing but the Creator Himself, nothing but Him remains in his heart, and all things speak to him, with the tongue of their state, declaring 'Hear my testimony before Him Who created all things in the finest of forms. I am the handiwork of God, Best of Creators… Then the lights of knowledge, truth, sincerity and love then flow from his heart as the light flows from the sun.'[45]

One last author who cannot be overlooked here, in view of his stature and the extent of his influence, is Shaykh Aḥmad Ibn 'Aṭā' Allāh al-Iskandarī (d. 709/1310). His *Kitāb al-Ḥikam*, a collection of teachings in the form of maxims on the spiritual path, is generally regarded as one of the classics of Sufism. Moreover it is by its very nature designed to be 'food for thought' and to stimulate reflection in the disciple, and a considerable number of commentaries on *al-Ḥikam al-'Aṭā'iyya* have been composed by other Sufi shaykhs. There are later works in the same genre which regrettably cannot be discussed here.

According to one of the first *ḥikam* or maxims in the book (12),[46] 'Nothing is more beneficial for the heart than seclusion (*'uzla*) in which it enters the arena of contemplation (*fikra*).' One of the best-known commentators, Shaykh Aḥmad Zarrūq, regards such seclusion as indispensable to successful reflection. Another maxim (29),[47] by contrast, opens up a whole dimension of spirituality, one

44 Abū Naṣr al-Sarrāj, *Kitāb al-Luma' fī al-taṣawwuf*, ed. R.A. Nicholson, 2nd ed. (London, 1963), p. 69.

45 Ibn al-Qayyim al-Jawziyya, *Madārij al-sālikīn*, ed. 'Abd al-Mun'im al-Ṣāliḥ (UAE, n.d.), p. 632. Translation by Malik Badri, *Contemplation*, p. 85.

46 The numbers given here are taken from the translation by Victor Danner, p. 25, and the commentary by Shaykh Aḥmad Zarrūq (*al-Sharḥ al-Ḥādī 'Ashar*, pp. 43-44). In *ḥikma* 12, the word *maydān*, here rendered as 'arena' and glossed by Zarrūq as 'a place where horses are exercised' was perhaps chosen as a counterpoint to the sense of concentration and/or confinement that is implicit in *'uzla* (seclusion).

47 Tr. Danner, p. 28; *Sharḥ*, pp. 75-77.

that should not be overlooked altogether even in this book which focuses on the primarily mental process of *tafakkur*. It throws into sharp relief the disparity between experiential knowledge of God, *maʿrifa*, which is acquired by unveiling (*kashf*), and knowledge (*ʿilm*) which is acquired by rational thought. (Ibn al-ʿArabī, whose entire theosophy is centred on *kashf*, or 'unveiling,' goes further, characterising *tafakkur* as a *balā*', a necessary process that is nonetheless a trial and temptation for mankind because of the uncertainty of a correct outcome.)[48] 'How vast is the difference between one who proceeds from God in his reasoning, and one who proceeds to Him by inference! One whose starting-point is Him knows God as He is, and proves their point with reference to Him as the Origin. Inductive reasoning arises from the lack of 'unitive connection' with Him. Otherwise, when was He ever absent, that one should need to proceed to Him by inference? And when was He ever distant, that phenomenal entities should unitively connect us to Him?'

By contrast, another *ḥikma* (85)[49] focuses on contemplation as a potential key to profound understanding: 'Outwardly all realms of being (*akwān*) are illusory, but inwardly they are indicative [of inner meanings] (*ʿibra*); hence the self looks at their outward, illusory aspect, while the heart looks at their indicative, inward aspect.' In a third maxim, with which this discussion must conclude, Ibn ʿAṭā' Allāh highlights the role of contemplation, observing (231) that 'Beneficial knowledge is that whose light-ray expands in the mind and removes the veil over the heart.'

Assessing Ghazālī's treatment of contemplation

As we have seen, Imam Ghazālī's treatment in the *Iḥyā*' of the art of contemplation has been highly influential and may well be widely

48 W.C. Chittick, *The Sufi Path of Knowledge: Ibn al-ʿArabi's Metaphysics of Imagination*, pp. 162-163, quoting from *al-Futūḥāt al-Makkiyya*. Ibn al-ʿArabī goes on to contend that rational thought can only show humans and the jinn what God is not like. To know what He is like one must have recourse to Revelation, whereas other created things possess innate and inspired direct knowledge (*maʿrifa*) of Him; which is why they glorify Him..

49 Tr. Danner, p. 36; *al-Sharḥ al-Ḥādī ʿAshar*, pp. 152-153.

regarded as wholly definitive. Nevertheless, it is legitimate to ask whether it covers its subject matter to as wide an extent as other Books of the *Iḥyā'* cover theirs. What, if anything, is missing, and does one need also to look in other sources to complete the picture?

In the first place, it is understandable, and inevitable, that most if not all, of the more esoteric aspects of the subject are not covered in *Kitāb al-Tafakkur*. The author states clearly in the *Iḥyā'*, in various contexts, that it is not his purpose to discuss matters that fall within the scope of *'ilm al-mukāshafa*, the knowledge of 'unveiling', with which some aspects of *tafakkur* can be said to be connected. That is probably at least one of the reasons why Najm al-Dīn Rāzī, one of the great Sufi authors of the Kubrawī Order, claimed that Ghazālī's *Kitāb 'Aja'ib al-qalb* (The Book of Wonders of the Heart), Book 21 of *Iḥyā' 'ulūm al-Dīn*, does not cover one-tenth of the subject. Concerning the nature of the heart – and this does relate to the matter of reflection with the heart – Rāzī states that just as the physical body has outward-directed senses, the heart too has senses which are analogous to them. He then proceeds to describe the five aspects or senses of the subtle heart and their functions. When the heart is completely pure and healthy, each of its five aspects will perform its appointed function of service in accordance with the Divine Command.[50] There is far more to be said about the esoteric aspects of contemplation, but for present purposes this must suffice.

Contemplation and Invocation

Secondly, many authorities on Sufism in Ghazālī's time and the following two centuries attach importance to the relationship between *fikr* (thought) and *dhikr* (invocation). It is not that Ghazālī fails to give due consideration to *dhikr* in its own right. Indeed, in Book 9 of the *Iḥyā'*, *Kitāb al-Adhkār wa al-Da'awāt* (Invocations and Supplications) where he shows *du'ā* (supplicatory prayer) to be a form of *fikr* as well as one of *dhikr*, he identifies five meanings,

50 Najm al-Dīn Rāzī, *Mirṣād al-'ibād*, ed. Muḥammad Amīn Riyāḥī (Tehran, 1352/1973, pp. 194-198; cf. *The Path of God's Bondsmen from Origin to Return*, tr. Hamid Algar (Delmar, NY 1982), pp. 207-210.

or modes, of *dhikr*: (i) striving to keep God always in one's mind; (ii) remembering and reflecting on (we have here a form of *fikr* classed as *dhikr*) other religious matters, not God Himself, such as death and the Afterlife; (iii) the repeated invocation of a Divine Name or formula; (iv) a state of permanent 'presence' in which no thought or concern remains for anything but God; and (v) a mode of invocation so intense that the invoker (*dhākir*) becomes entirely permeated by the Invoked (*Madhkūr*).[51]

Ghazālī also says that 'The benefits of *duʿā'* as an act of contemplation include the habitual reminder or realisation that one's fate at any moment of life is in the hands of the Creator, upon Whom one is utterly dependent. Because there are appropriate formulae of prayer and remembrance for every event or occasion, each instant of one's existence offers the opportunity to recall the underlying reality of the human situation and to petition for Divine Blessings and Mercy.'

For some authors, the two are complementary and one will not yield its full fruits without the other. For some, *fikr* (or *tafakkur*) in the technical sense cannot be safely embarked on until the disciple has advanced some distance on the Path. A suitable example to illustrate this is another master from Khurāsān, Shaykh Aḥmad-i Jām (d. 535/1141-2). Section (*faṣl*) 6 of one of his treatises, *Ḥadīqat al-ḥaqīqa* ('The Garden of Reality', not to be confused with Sanā'ī's great poem), tackles the relationship between *dhikr* and *fikr*, and expresses a cautious approach regarding the latter:

> 'We now come to the question of what is best, of *fikr* and *firāsat* (intuition), and the origin and nature of *khiyāl* (imagination). For those in the material realm (*ʿālam-i arkān*), *dhikr* is superior to *dhikr*. 'Invocation is the provision of the lover in his search for the Beloved.' Whoever inhabits the spiritual realm (*ʿālam-i bāṭin*) and has knowledge of the heart, *fikr* is better for him than *dhikr*, for "Reflection is the heart's guard against drowning in the sea of forgetfulness." In the material world, *dhikr* can assume forms, since *dhikr* is on the tongue and the tongue is a material entity. *Fikr*, on the other hand, does not

51 *Invocations & Supplications*: Kitāb al-adhkār wa'l-daʿawāt, introduction, pp. xxi-xxviii.

> coalesce in forms; *fikr* is in the heart, and he [the seeker still in the material world] has not attained to the heart. It is better for him to perform *dhikr*. It is not appropriate, at this stage, for him to perform *fikr* as a [regular] imposition (*ba-takalluf*), for the heart has yet to be illumined by the lights of contemplating the Spiritual World. He is not yet free from the bonds and prison of the lower self, the lower world, desire, and Satan; nor has love of rank and wealth removed itself from his vision. For the seeker to practice contemplation at this stage would be like a man setting out on a dark, cloudy night, on a route unknown and unfamiliar. However far he might go, it would count as though he had not gone (*na-rafta buwad*). It would be a rare event if he went aright, and "there is no rule governing the exception"; he may get lost in this manner. He cannot come by the road unless he endures much suffering. Such a journey is better not made at all. ...As God Most High has said, "Enter houses by their doors."[52] Invocation with the tongue is the key that opens the door to heart's meditation; should one lose the key, the door will never be opened.'[53]

In addition to the few sources cited here there exists in the literature of Islamic spirituality a rich vein of wisdom concerning the complementary roles of *dhikr* and *fikr*. Admittedly, Ghazālī does touch on this topic a number of times in the *Iḥyā'* - K. Nakamura cites as examples the Book on Prayer (*Kitāb Asrār al-Ṣalāt, bāb* 7) and the Book of Litanies (*Kitāb Tartīb al-Awrād, bāb* 1)[54] – and he avers that adding *dhikr* to *fikr* will help by reinforcing in the heart the knowledge gained by *fikr*. However, nothing is said on the matter in Book 39, where it would have been a valuable addition. Perhaps, despite the author's prodigious powers of organisation, the necessary compartmentalisation of subjects into separate Books in the *Iḥyā'* at times militates against a more holistic presentation of such matters. In any case, it is a tried and tested fact that one of the fruits

---

52 From Qur'ān 2:189.

53 This is an excerpt from the passage in *Ḥadīqat al-ḥaqīqa*, ed. Muḥammad 'Alī Muwaḥḥid, pp. 148-149.

54 See *Invocations & Supplications*: Kitāb al-adhkār wa'l-da'awāt, *Book IX of The Revival of the Religious Sciences*, tr. K. Nakamura (Cambridge, 1990), p. xxiii, xxxix.

of persistent, methodical invocation, as prescribed (in accordance with the Prophetic *Sunna*) by the masters quoted here, is to produce in the heart a light, a clarity, and finally an experiential certainty which eliminates the risk of misapprehensions and *khawāṭir* or thought-impulses of the wrong kind taking hold. Jalāl al-Dīn Rūmī, who has far more to say about invocation than contemplation, says about Sufis:

> 'They have polished their bosoms in invocation and contemplation, that the heart's mirror may receive fresh, integral (lit. 'virgin') images.'[55]

Contemplation and Imagination

At the beginning of the passage quoted above concerning *dhikr* and *fikr* Aḥmad-i Jām mentions the faculty of imagination. Now, the connection between imagination, understood as the mental representation of an object, and reflection is another theme deserving of consideration. For one thing, reflection on a subject that presents itself as abstract, however tangible its connotations, depends on the mind being able to 'envisage' such things. According to Albert Einstein, 'Imagination is more important than knowledge. For knowledge is limited to all we now know and understand, while imagination embraces the entire world, and all there ever will be to know and understand.' In the nature of things, the more vividly the imagination is able to 'represent' them, the more readily will the act of contemplation have strong and lasting effects. In past centuries, when it was almost impossible for people's minds to be saturated by visual images, the imaginative faculty that is innate in mankind was not normally stunted or atrophied in the ways so often manifested today. Listening to recitation of the eschatological verses of the Qur'ān, for example, would often transport the listener to a state in which they could be described as virtually witnessing them. That is still possible in our time, of course; but if the phenomenon

---

55 Rūmī, *Mathnawī*, *Daftar* 1, *bayt* 3154: *Books I-II: Text*, ed. R.A. Nicholson (London, 1925), p. 194; *Books I-II: Translation*, tr. R.A. Nicholson (London, 1926), p. 172.

just described is compared with the present-day concept of 'virtual reality' it is easy to see that there has been a great and consequential impoverishment of the human imagination. In this context we are of course considering imagination in its positive aspects, and in the context of spirituality there are other dimensions of imagination that are of immense interest but lie beyond the scope of our subject, pertaining as they do to the realm of *mukāshafa*.[56]

The one thing that is too crucial to be left unsaid here is that from the viewpoint of the hierarchical levels of Being, the Imaginal in the sense of sensible similitudes and archetypes is more real than the concrete, tangible world around us. As Jalāl al-Dīn Rūmī puts it, in one of his Discourses: 'This world is sustained by imagination (*khiyāl*). You call this world "reality" because it can be seen and perceived; and you call those inner realities (*ma'ānī*) of which the world is an offshoot "imagination." [But] the opposite is the case. It is this world that is imagination, for that inner reality produces a hundred [worlds] like this one – which then decay, fall into ruin, and vanish - and then it produces a new world which is better and never grows old, transcending newness and oldness...'[57]

We have also, however, to deal with imagination in the negative sense: that is, in the form of illusion and delusion, of which there is no shortage in today's cognitive and spiritual landscape. In the past, a far greater receptiveness and sensitivity could be assumed, and it may be doubted whether al-Muḥāsibī, when writing *Kitāb al-Tawahhum*, or al- Ghazālī, when writing *Kitāb al-Tafakkur*, had to consider making allowances for a possible deficiency of that kind in their readers. In the 21st century, however, it is a problem which partially or wholly obstructs the ability to see beyond that which is readily accessible to our minds because of predisposition and/or experience. That in turn has consequences such as (to give but two

---

56 For example, Muḥyī al-Dīn Ibn al-'Arabī's theories concerning the progression in visionary experience (*istiḥḍār khayālī*): first refining the faculty of imagination to gain mental visions in the form of 'likenesses' (*tamthīl*), then dream visions (*ru'yā*), then vision with the heart or the 'inner eye' (*baṣīra*). In the last of these, Ibn al-'Arabī contends, the human becomes the mirror in which God beholds Himself. See Henry Corbin, *Creative Imagination in the Ṣūfism of Ibn 'Arabī* (Princeton, 1969), pp. 231-232.

57 Jalāl al-Dīn Rūmī, *Fīh mā fīh*, ed. Badī' al-Zamān Furūzānfar (Tehran, 1348 sh./1969), p. 120.

examples) refusal to admit to previous errors in one's thinking, and a shortage or even an absence of empathy towards other people and their situation, feelings and motivations. Admittedly Imam Ghazālī does not give consideration in Book 39 to reflection on non-religious matters; he explicitly deems that to be an activity devoid of any benefit. He does, however, enjoin recalling and evaluating one's own actions. Common experience teaches us that this is an area where human nature permits us to err in our judgement as well as our memory, a fact which leads into the next, and the final, point to be made in assessing the scope of *Kitāb al-Tafakkur*.

Contemplation and verification (*taḥqīq*)

In our consideration of *Kitāb al-Tafakkur* and its scope, its more esoteric aspects and its relationship with invocation and imagination have now been touched upon. There remains, however, one further point that deserves further mention, which is part of what is implicit in Shaykh Aḥmad-i Jām's assessment and is also related to the concerns for sound and reasoning evidenced in the work of Abū Zayd al-Balkhī. Ghazālī has introduced and expounded a methodology of contemplation which is a key means to self-knowledge and knowledge of God. In fact, he states in Book 39 that *tafakkur* which is not directed towards acquiring knowledge is devoid of value. The process of logical reasoning which his methodology insists upon can only be relied on to give correct results if the starting-point and premises are factually and/or morally valid and, additionally, the reasoning is sound. 'A proper adjustment to reality can only be achieved when reality is correctly perceived.'[58] Otherwise, a process designed to bring truthful knowledge, serenity and, ultimately, states and actions conducive to salvation (being one of the *Iḥyā*'s ten *Munjiyyāt*, or means of deliverance) may instead bring misguidance, disturbance, and in extreme cases the risk of perdition. It must be remembered that Ghazālī's counsel in the *Iḥyā'* is directed towards ordinary believers as well as initiates.

---

58 Abraham J. Twerski, *The Spiritual Self* (Center City, MI, 2000), p. 23.

Suppose, for example, that X is conscious of having committed a sin, but then finds hope and consolation – as many Muslims surely have done – in the Hadith about a prostitute who was forgiven and earned Paradise by giving a drink of water to a dog.[59] It is not inconceivable that X could reason as follows: (i) the prostitute may have spent her entire adult life sinning every day (whereas I have only one sin to worry about); (ii) she was forgiven and saved from Hell by showing kindness to a dog (a lower life form than a human); therefore (iii) if I show an equivalent or greater kindness to a human being (giving them a glass of water, perhaps, or even a bottle), that will certainly make my prospects of salvation greater than those of the prostitute.' All of this is logical but ignores the possibility that various factors apply that would invalidate X's assumptions and imperil his eternal happiness. Conversely, it is not difficult to imagine a scenario in which Y, who is a pessimist rather than an optimist, uses reasoning to lose all hope, and thereby to arrive at a 'no win' appraisal of their existential situation. An atheist may reason that (i) humankind rely upon their senses to perceive things; (ii) the existence of God cannot be perceived by the human senses; therefore (iii) God cannot exist (*quod absit*). And so on. What is known as 'the scientific method' of investigation necessarily entails a process of 'feedback' and verification through experimental findings and in the light of other information that becomes available. This process, in the nature of things, requires time, patience, and persistence. Ordinary Muslims, too, need to check themselves (and, when appropriate, each other) for cognitive bias, and check on the validity of their conclusions to the extent their capabilities permit. This does not mean that vacillation and indecision are called for, and circumstances often do not permit a long delay. The best way in all matters being the middle way, one must guard against false uncertainty as well as false certainty, since one can only do one's best, and then be resolute, trusting in God, the All-Knowing, the All-Merciful, Who is well aware of our weaknesses and failings.

As a theologian, philosopher and jurist, Imam Abū Ḥāmid al-Ghazālī was acutely aware of the importance of rigorously logical thought. His intention was to enable Muslims to stand on their own

59 Al-Bukhārī, *Ṣaḥīḥ*, Hadith 3143; Muslim, *Ṣaḥīḥ*, Hadith 2245.

two feet as far as reasonably and safely possible, with a confidence and serenity made possible by a firm footing in the theory and practice of the *Dīn*. Accordingly, he might perhaps have accepted the idea that verification be added to his methodology of acquiring knowledge, wisdom, and virtue by means of contemplation: CONTEMPLATION > CONCLUSION > VERIFICATION > KNOWLEDGE > STATE > ACTION > STATE.

In conclusion

Imam Abū Ḥāmid al-Ghazālī's masterly presentation of the merits and methodology of the art of reflection has rarely, if ever, been needed more than it is in our times, when there are so many factors that impede us from 'taking time out' to think. John Milton, in his poem *Comus*, expresses this rather better, and in a vein recalling that of Sanā'ī:

> '…And Wisdom's self
> oft seeks to sweet retired solitude,
> where, with her best nurse, Contemplation,
> She plumes her feathers, and lets grow her wings,
> that in the various bustle of resort
> were all too ruffled, and sometimes impaired.'[60]

The situation cannot be said to be easier today than it was in the days of the author of *Paradise Lost*. Faced with an almost constant barrage of (partly self-imposed) distractions and opportunities (or pressure) to 'multi-task', we may well find ourselves at risk of caving in and letting the course of events wash over us, so that we lead by default an 'unexamined life' – the kind that Socrates, according to Plato's *Apologia*, described as 'not worth living'. Thank God, then, that one of the greatest minds of the Islamicate world – and indeed of all time – is at our disposal to offer guidance and direct us towards contemplation of that which truly matters now and will matter until the end of Time.

---

60 John Milton, 'Comus'. In *The English Poems of John Milton* (World's Classics), London 1940, pp. 40-70; see p. 53.

This translation is based on the Arabic edition published by Dār al-Minhāj of Jeddah in 2011. The content of the footnotes relating to the sources of Hadiths is taken from the classic reference work on the *takhrīj* of Hadiths in the *Iḥyā'*, al-Zabīdī's *Itḥāf al-sādat al-muttaqīn* and/or from the Dār al-Minhāj edition. Special recognition and thanks are due to the late Father Giuseppe Celentano, who produced the first Western-language translation, in Italian, of *Kitāb al-Tafakkur*;[61] both his understanding of the text and his annotations have been helpful to the writer. Regrettably, the French translation by H. Boutaleb and A.-W. Gouraud was not obtainable in time for me to benefit from it.

Heartfelt thanks are due to the following for their invaluable encouragement and assistance: 'Abd al-Samad Yahya Paolo Urizzi, the publisher of Fr. Celentano's translation, who long ago presented me with a signed copy which I still treasure; Ustadh Amjad Tarsin, Shaykh Yahya Rhodus, and Ustadh Hasan Petrus; and Aisha Gray Henry and Neville Blakemore of Fons Vitae, who accepted this work for publication and have shown great thoughtfulness and forbearance. The mistakes and infelicities are my responsibility alone.

This translation and introductory essay are dedicated to the loving memory of my parents, Daniel and Pamela Waley (1921-2017), both of whom were born a century ago this year. Although my thinking was to depart from theirs in so many respects, they taught and encouraged me to reason and to reflect. In that respect, and in a myriad other ways that I am still coming to realise, I owe them a debt that never could be repaid.

Let the concluding words be from the Book which of all books is most deserving of contemplation by those seeking wisdom and understanding: '*Say: "One thing only I enjoin upon you: to stand up for God, in pairs or singly, and to take thought."*' (34:46). '*And those are the symbols We devise for mankind, that they may perhaps reflect.*' (59:21) '*And whoever is granted wisdom has indeed been granted immense good.*' (2:269).

And God knows best.

---

61 Al-Ghazālī, *Il Libro della Meditazione*. Trieste: Società Italiana Testi Islamici, 1988.

THE BOOK OF CONTEMPLATION

1

Preface

In the Name of God, the All-Merciful, the Most Merciful

[ALL] praise be to God, Who has ordained no direction or location wherein His Glory might be delimited. Nor has He set up for the stairways of the feet of the imagination or the range of the arrows of [human] understanding any course [by which] to [reach] the sanctuary of his Greatness. Rather He has left the hearts of those who seek [Him] bedazzled and bewildered in the wilderness of His Magnificence. Whenever they move in an attempt to arrive at their goal, they are forcibly driven back by the sublime splendours of [Divine] Majesty. Yet when they are on the point of leaving in despair, there issues from the pavilions of [Divine] Beauty the call, 'Patience, patience!'

[The seekers] are then told, 'Give yourselves over to thinking upon the lowly station of servitude. Were you to reflect upon the Majesty of the Divine Lord you could not reckon It rightly. If you seek a subject beyond your own attributes on which to reflect, behold the gifts and bounties of God, Exalted is He: how they are brought to you in ceaseless succession. Then renew your remembrance of God and your thankfulness to Him for each one of those benefits. Reflect upon the oceans of Divine Acts of Providence: see how they pour out over the Universe [bringing] goodness and badness, gain and harm, hardship and ease, triumph and utter loss, repair and ruin, concealment and divulgation, faith and disbelief, acknowledgement and denial. If you [each one of you] then pass on from the contemplation of [Divine] Actions to that of the [Divine] Essence, you are attempting something unspeakable; indeed, you are endangering your very soul in that you wrongfully and outrageously [purpose to] transgress the bounds of human capacity. For [all human] intellects, even before they can receive their first illuminations, are overwhelmed, reduced to abject retreat by the all-compelling force of [God's] Irresistible Might.'

Exaltation and abundant salutation be upon Muhammad, Master of the Children of Adam, though that Mastership is not [to be] counted as a boast.[1] May that exaltation endure as a provision and a treasure for us in the Courtyards of the [Mustering after] Resurrection; and upon his House and Companions, every one of whom arose in the firmament of the Faith as a [radiant] full moon and a leader to the [various] groups of Muslims.

To commence. It is related in the *Sunna* that 'An hour of reflection is better than a year of worship.'[2] In the Book of God Most High, too, are many exhortations to ponder, consider, assess, and reflect. It is evident also that reflection is the key to gaining illumination, the basis for insight, the net for catching forms of knowledge, and the snare for trapping direct perception and understanding. Most of mankind are aware of its merit and its importance; but they are ignorant of its true nature, its fruits, where it should begin from and where it can lead to, the way to practice it and the extent of its scope. Nor do they know how, on what, or for what purpose to contemplate, or what is [to be] sought by contemplation. Is it an end in itself or [sought] to gain some result from which to benefit? And if it be for some result, what is that result? Is it some [kind of]

1 A Hadith found in the following sources: Abū Nuʿaym al-Iṣfahānī, *Ḥilyat al-awliyā'*; Iṣbahānī, *al-Targhīb wa al-tarhīb*; al-Ṭabarānī, *al-Awsaṭ*. Variants with slightly different wording but identical purport are also related by Bayhaqī, *Shuʿab al-īmān* (from Ibn ʿUmar), Abū al-Shaykh (from Ibn ʿAbbās), and others.

2 The source of this particular Tradition has not been traced. Very similar Traditions are found in al-ʿIrāqī, *al-Jawāhir wa al-durar* (narrated from Ibn ʿAbbās), and Abū al-Shaykh, *al-ʿAẓama* (from Abū Hurayra). The intention is to show that the wonders and vastness of Creation themselves extend beyond the range of the human imagination.

knowledge, or [spiritual] state, or both? It is important to reveal [answers to] the whole of that [series of questions]. If God Most High wills, we shall first discuss the merits of reflection; then the true nature and fruits of reflection; and then the subjects and fields [suitable] for reflection.

2

The merit of contemplation

God, Exalted is He, has commanded us in innumerable passages of His Mighty Scripture to reflect and to ponder. He, Exalted is He, has praised those who contemplate, saying, *'Those who remember God standing, sitting, and reclining, and reflect upon the creation of the Heavens and the Earth: "Dear Lord, not in vain did You create this!"'*[1] Ibn 'Abbās,[2] may God be well-pleased with him and his father, observed: 'There was a group of people who reflected upon God, Mighty and Glorious is He.' In response the Emissary of God, may God exalt and preserve him, said, 'Reflect upon God's creation, but do not reflect upon God; for you cannot reckon Him at His true measure.'[3]

It is also related that the Prophet, blessings and peace be upon him, went out one day to see a group of people, and they were engaged in contemplation. 'How is it,' he enquired, 'that you are not speaking to one another?' They replied, 'We are reflecting upon the Creation that God has made, Mighty and Glorious is He.' 'Then do so,' replied [the Prophet]. 'Reflect upon God's Creation; do not

---

1 Qur'ān 3:191.

2 'Abd Allāh ibn 'Abbās (d. 68/687), was the cousin of the Prophet and one of the most erudite of his Companions. He is revered and cited most particularly as a commentator on the meanings of the Qur'ān.

3 Not in the canonical Hadith sources, but found in the following sources, according to the Dār al-Minhāj edition of the *Iḥyā'*: al-Kharkūshī (Persian: Khargūshī), *Tahdhīb al-asrār*, p. 693; Abū al-Shaykh, *al-'Aẓama*, 2; al-Bayhaqī, *al-Asmā' wa al-ṣifāt*, pp. 271, 389); Abū Nu'aym al-Iṣfahānī, *Ḥilya*, vol. 6, p. 66, from a Hadith narrated by 'Abd Allāh ibn Salām; al-Bayhaqī, *Shu'ab al-īmān*, 119.

reflect upon Him. To the West of here lies a white land whose light is its own whiteness and whose whiteness is its own light, and the sun takes forty days to traverse it. It is peopled by creatures of God who have never for one instant disobeyed Him.' 'In that case, Emissary of God,' they asked, 'how does Satan stand in relation to them?' Said [the Prophet], 'They are not aware [even] whether or not Satan has been created.' '[Are they] from the Children of Adam?' they asked. He replied, 'They are not aware [even] whether or not Adam has been created.'[4]

'Aṭā'[5] related the following: 'One day I went with 'Ubayd ibn 'Umayr[6] to [visit] 'Ā'isha,[7] may God be pleased with her. She spoke with us, and there was a screen between her and us. "'Ubayd", she asked, "what inhibits you from visiting us?" He replied, "It is the fact that the Emissary [of God], may God exalt and preserve him, said "Visit people [only] at intervals, so that the affection [between you] may increase." Ibn 'Umayr then asked [her]: "Do tell us about the most extraordinary thing that you saw the Emissary of God do, may God exalt and preserve him." ['Ā'isha] wept and said, "Everything about him was extraordinary! [Once] he came to me, on the night allotted to me, and his skin even touched mine. Then he said, 'Leave me to worship my Lord, Mighty and Glorious is He.' Thereupon he arose to [go to] the waterskin and performed the ablution [from it]. He then stood up in prayer, weeping until his beard was soaking wet, and prostrated himself until the ground was soaked. After that, he lay down on his side until Bilāl[8] came to call him to the dawn

---

4 Not in the canonical Hadith sources, but found in the following works, according to the Dār al-Minhāj edition of the *Iḥyā'*: al-Kharkūshī, *Tahdhīb al-asrār*, p. 693; Abū al-Shaykh, *al-'Aẓama*, 953, as a *marfū'* Hadith; al-Daylamī, *Musnad al-Firdaws* 708, from a Hadith related by Ibn 'Abbās; Ibn al-Jawzī, *al-Muntaẓam*, vol. 1, p. 61.

5 'Aṭā' ibn Abī Rabāḥ (d. 114/732) was a Follower (*Ṭābi'ī*), i.e. a member of the next generation of Muslims after the Companions). Noted as a jurist and as a Hadith transmitter, he served as Muftī of Mecca.

6 'Ubayd ibn 'Umayr ibn Qatāda al-Laythī (dates unknown) was one of the story-tellers of Mecca.

7 'Ā'isha bint Abī Bakr (d. 58/678), favourite wife of the Prophet, and one of the most important transmitters of Hadiths.

8 Bilāl ibn Rabāḥ (d. ca. 20/641), an Abyssinian slave freed by Abū Bakr, was an early convert and among the most revered Companions. He was very dear to the Prophet, who appointed him as the *mu'adhdhin* or caller to prayer of Islam's first mosque, one of the actions which proclaimed his opposition to racism.

prayer. [Bilāl] asked, "O Emissary of God, what is it that has made you weep, when God has already forgiven you '*your sins, past and future*'?"[9] "Come now, Bilāl!" he replied, "What is there to prevent me from weeping? This past night, God Most High has revealed to me that '*Truly in the creation of the heavens and the earth and the alternation of night and day are portents for those with discernment.*'"[10] [God's Envoy] then added: "Woe to anyone who recites this without reflecting upon it!'"[11]

Al-Awzāʿī[12] was asked, 'What is the purpose (*ghāya*) of reflecting upon [these words]?' He replied, 'To recite them and to exercise one's intellect upon them.'[13]

It is recounted on the authority of Muḥammad ibn Wasiʿ[14] that two men from Basra made a journey to see (*rakibā ilā*) Umm Dharr after the death of Abū Dharr,[15] and asked her about Abū Dharr's devotions. She told them that he used to spend whole days in contemplation in one part of the house.

It is reported of al-Ḥasan [al-Baṣrī][16] that he affirmed that

---

9 Qur'ān 48:2.

10 Qur'ān 3:190.

11 According to al-Zabīdī's commentary on the *Iḥyā'*, *Itḥāf al-sāda* (vol. 10, p. 163), this Hadith is found in the *Ṣaḥīḥ* of Ibn Ḥibbān, and also in Ibn Abī al-Dunyā, Ibn 'Asākir and others, as related from 'Aṭā' by 'Abd al-Malik ibn Abī Sulaymān. It is also cited in al-Kharkūshī, *Tahdhīb al-asrār*, p. 694.

12 'Abd al-Raḥmān ibn 'Amr al-Awzāʿī (d/ 157/774), a jurist from what is now Lebanon, founded a *madhhab* or legal school which in the 3rd/9th century was supplanted, largely by the Mālikī school.

13 This saying, and all but one of the sayings quoted by Ghazālī in this section of the Book from this point onwards, are found in al-Kharkūshī, *Tahdhīb al-asrār*, pp. 694-698.

14 Probably Muḥammad ibn Wāsiʿ al-'Azdī (d. ca. 132/750), a Follower famous for his *zuhd* (abstinence) who was also a jurist and Hadith expert. Celentano (p. 27), however, identifies him as Abū Bakr Muḥammad ibn Wāsiʿ al-Baṣrī (d. 123/741), who also was a jurist and an ascetic.

15 Abū Dharr al-Ghifārī (d. ca. 31/652) was an eminent Companion of the Prophet, from whom he transmitted a great many Hadiths. Umm Dharr (dates unknown) was his widow.

16 Born in Medina, al-Ḥasan al-Baṣrī (d. 110/728), of Baṣra in Iraq, became one of the outstanding and influential figures among the *Tābiʿūn* or Followers. A preacher, ascetic, theologian and Qur'ān commentator, al-Ḥasan also features in the *silsila* or spiritual genealogy of a number of Sufi Orders. In Book 23 of the *Iḥyā'* Ghazālī reports al-Ḥasan as having related as a Hadith (though it is not found in canonical sources), that 'Reflection is half of worship, while eating frugally is all of it.' See *Al-Ghazālī On Disciplining the Soul & On Breaking the Two Desires*, tr. T.J. Winter, p. 108.

'Reflecting for one hour[17] is better than spending all night [in worship].'

Al-Fuḍayl [ibn 'Iyāḍ][18] is said to have observed: 'Reflection is a mirror in which you can observe your good and bad actions.'

Ibrāhīm [ibn Ad-ham][19] was told, 'You spend too much time in contemplation (*fikra*).' He replied, 'Contemplation is the very marrow of action.'[20]

Sufyān ibn 'Uyayna[21] often used to repeat as a proverb these words [in verse]:

'If a man be given to contemplation,
in all things there is a lesson for him.'

It is related of Ṭā'ūs[22] that he said: 'The Apostles asked Jesus, son of Mary, "O Spirit of God, is there anyone like you upon Earth today?" [Jesus] replied: "Yes: he whose speech is remembrance (*dhikr*), whose silence is contemplation (*fikr*), and whose vision (*naẓar*) is cognisance (*'ibra*) – such a one resembles me."'

Al-Ḥasan [al-Baṣrī] observed: 'If a man's speech is not wisdom, it is vain talk; if his silence is not reflection, it is error; and if his seeing is not taking note (*i'tibār*), it is frivolity.' [Al-Ḥasan] also interpreted [God's] Words, Exalted is He, '*I will turn away from My Signs those who act with arrogance in the world without just cause*'[23] [as follows]: 'I will prevent their hearts from reflecting about Me.'

It is reported that Abū Sa'īd al-Khudrī[24] stated: 'The Emissary of

---

17 The word used here, *sā'a*, can also be translated as 'a moment' or 'a while', and that may well be what the Prophet intended, since timepieces measuring hours precisely were of course unknown in his time.

18 Al-Fuḍayl ibn 'Iyāḍ (d. 187/803), a native of Khurāsān (northeastern Iran), was by some accounts a highway robber before he repented and became a devout and learned ascetic.

19 Ibrāhīm ibn Ad-ham (d. 161/777), the son of a local ruler or governor in western Central Asia, was one of the most noted, and quoted, Sufis of the 2nd/8th century.

20 Reading, with Celentano, *al-'amal* (action) rather than *al-'aql* (intellect).

21 Sufyān ibn 'Uyayna al-Hilālī al-Kūfī (107-198/725-814) was a distinguished jurist and authority on Qur'ān and Hadith sciences.

22 Ṭā'ūs ibn Kaysān al-Yamānī (d. 150/767), a Tābi'ī or Follower, was an ethnically Persian native of Yemen. He was a major authority on, and transmitter of, Hadiths.

23 Qur'ān 7:146.

24 Abū Sa'īd Sa'd ibn Mālik al-Khazrajī al-Khudrī (d. 74/693), a Companion, spent his whole life in Medina and is numbered among the *Anṣār* or 'Helpers' from that city who made immense sacrifices to help the cause of Islam. This weak Hadith

God, may God exalt and preserve him, said, "Grant your eyes their share in worshipping." "Emissary of God," he was asked, "what is their share in worshipping?" He replied, "It is looking into the Holy Book (*Muṣḥaf*), reflecting upon it, and taking note of the wonders that it contains.'"

Again, a woman who dwelt in the desert near Mecca is said to have observed: 'If the hearts of the godly (*muttaqīn*) were able to realise in their reflections what bounties of the Afterlife have already been stored up for them behind the veils of the Unseen, never again could they occupy themselves with life in this world, or take any delight in this world.'

Luqmān[25] was wont to spend long periods sitting in solitude. His master would pass by him and say, 'Luqmān, you are constantly sitting by yourself. If only you would sit with people, that would be more sociable for you.' To this Luqmān would reply, 'Prolonged solitude enhances the understanding gained by contemplation, and prolonged contemplation is a guide on the path to Paradise.'

Said Wahb ibn Munabbih:[26] 'Never did a man ponder at length without gaining knowledge, or [truly] know without [performing] actions [accordingly].'

'Umar ibn 'Abd al-'Azīz[27] remarked that 'Reflecting upon the bounties of God, Great and Glorious is He, is among the preeminent acts of worship.'

'Abd Allāh ibn al-Mubārak[28] said one day to Sahl ibn 'Alī,[29] seeing

---

is related by al-Bayhaqī in *Shu'ab al-īmān*, no. 2030, and by al-Kharkūshī, p. 695.

25 Luqmān is a revered sage who is mentioned and quoted in Sūra 31 of the Qur'ān. This makes him a historical rather than a legendary figure to Muslims, but although there are many stories about him and he is often said to have been an Ethiopian slave, nothing certain is known about his life or his origins.

26 Wahb ibn Munabbih al-Dhimarī (d. ca. 110/728) was, like Ṭā'ūs, a Persian native of Yemen. A *Tābi'ī*, Wahb may have been a convert from Judaism. In any case, he is renowned as a wise and devout man and an authority on *Isrā'īliyyāt*, or Jewish traditions This saying sums up one of Ghazālī's key messages..

27 'Umar ibn 'Abd al-'Azīz (d. 101/720), the eighth caliph of the Umayyad dynasty, was exceptional among the rulers of his line, being famed for his justice, piety, scrupulosity and abstemiousness.

28 'Abd Allāh ibn al-Mubārak (d. 181/797) was a pious and learned individual from Khurāsān, and a leading authority on Hadith. He is also noted for his verses, wise sayings, and witticisms.

29 This individual has not been identified. The best-known men of that name,

him silently absorbed in contemplation, 'What point (*ayna*) have you reached?' 'The Traverse (*al-Sirāṭ*) [over Hell]', replied [Sahl].

According to Bishr [al-Ḥāfī],[30] 'If only people were to reflect upon the Supreme Immensity (*'Aẓama*) of God, they would not disobey God (Mighty and Glorious is He).'

Ibn 'Abbās is reported to have said: 'Two cycles of prayer, with a modicum of reflection, (*rak'atān muqtaṣidān fī tafakkur*) are better than an entire night's vigil [for worship] without [presence of] heart.'

Abū Shurayḥ[31] was walking along, then sat down. He veiled his face with his mantle and began to weep. 'Why are you weeping?' someone enquired. [Abū Shurayḥ] replied: 'I was thinking about the passing of my life, the paucity of my [good] deeds, and the approach of the hour of my death.'

Said Abū Sulaymān [al-Dārānī],[32] 'Accustom your eyes to weeping and your hearts to contemplation.' He also stated that 'Thinking about this world is a veil over the Next World and a punishment for those beloved of God (*ahl al-walāya*), whereas thinking about the Next World entails wisdom and brings hearts to life.'

Ḥātim [al-Aṣamm][33] declared: 'From consideration (*al-'ibra*) comes increase in knowledge; from remembrance (*dhikr*), increase in love; and from contemplation (*fikr*), increase in reverential fear (*khawf*) [of God].'

---

like the Hadith transmitter 'Alī ibn Sahl al-Dūrī, were not contemporary with Ibn al-Mubārak. In this anecdote the man in question was evidently engaged in meditation on the stages of the Last Day and the Judgement.

30 Bishr ibn al-Ḥārith al-Ḥāfī, 'the Barefoot' (d. 227/841-2) was born in the city of Marw (present-day Mary, Turkmenistan) but settled in Baghdad. Bishr is one of the eminent Sufi saints who are famous for having repented after having lived spectacularly sinful early lives.

31 Probably Abū Shurayḥ Khuwaylid ibn 'Amr al-Khuzā'ī (dates unknown), a Companion, who related one of the best-known Hadiths in Bukhārī's *al-Jāmi' al-Ṣaḥīḥ* (*Īmān*, 78).

32 Abū Sulaymān 'Abd al-Raḥmān ibn 'Aṭiyya al-Dārānī (d. 205/820 or 215/830) either was born or settled in a village near Damascus. His profound and original sayings on the doctrines and methods of the Sufi Path are quoted in many classical sources as authoritative.

33 Ḥātim ibn 'Alwān, known as Ḥātim al-Aṣamm, meaning 'the Deaf' (d. 237/851) was a famous Sufi saint from Balkh, in what is now northern Afghanistan, from whom numerous sayings have been recorded. For a longer saying of Ḥātim's regarding contemplation, beginning 'A believer is busy with reflection and perseverance,' see *Al-Ghazālī on Disciplining the Soul & on Breaking the Two Desires*, tr. T.J. Winter, pp. 69-70.

Said Ibn 'Abbās: 'Reflection upon goodness invites one to act upon it, and remorse over evildoing invites one to forsake it.'

It is related that God, Exalted is He, has declared in one of His Scriptures: 'I do not accept the words of every wise man, but I look into his concerns and his desires. If his concerns and desires are for Me, I make his silence contemplation and his speech thankful praise [of Me], even if he is not [physically] speaking.'

As al-Ḥasan [al-Baṣrī] remarked: 'People of intellect never cease to return through remembrance (*dhikr*) to contemplation (*fikr*) and through contemplation to remembrance, until they speak with their hearts, which speak with wisdom.'[34]

Isḥāq ibn Khalaf[35] narrated [the following]: 'Dā'ūd al-Ṭā'ī,[36] may God Most High be merciful to him, was sitting on a rooftop one moonlit night, reflecting upon *"the Dominion of the Heavens and Earth"*[37]. He looked at the sky and wept so [violently] that he fell onto a neighbour's house.' Isḥāq continued: 'So the owner of the house leapt out of bed, naked and sword in hand, imagining that it was a thief. When he saw Dā'ūd, he stepped back, put down the sword, and asked, "Whoever was it who flung you from the roof?" "That I did not notice" replied [Dā'ūd].'

Junayd[38] declared: 'The noblest and most elevated gatherings are sessions accompanied by reflection (*fikra*) in the field of [the doctrine of] Unity (*tawḥīd*); basking in the fragrance of the breezes of esoteric knowledge (*ma'rifa*); drinking of the ocean of intense love (*widād*) from the goblet of [Divine] Love; and contemplating (*naẓar*) God, Great and Glorious is He, with the best possible opinion.' Then he added, 'Ah, what glorious gatherings! What delectable wine!

34 This important teaching is among the earliest to indicate that rather than wondering or debating whether *dhikr* or *fikr* is the more important, one should see them as complementary.

35 This individual cannot be identified with certainty. The best-known person of that name died in or about 230/845 and so could not have narrated a story about Dā'ūd al-Ṭā'ī.

36 Dā'ūd ibn Nuṣayr al-Ṭā'ī (d. ca. 165/781), of Kūfa in Iraq, was a scholar and an influential Sufi shaykh.

37 Qur'ān 6:75 and 7:185.

38 Abū al-Qāsim al-Junayd of Baghdad (d. 298/910), a Sufi shaykh and jurist of Persian extraction, is one of the most celebrated and most often quoted of all authorities on Sufism.

Blessed is the one on whom it is bestowed!'

Said [Imām] al-Shāfiʿī[39], may God Most High be merciful to him: 'Make use of silence to enhance [your] discourse, and of contemplation to enhance [your powers of intellectual] discovery.'[40]

He also observed: 'Sound insight in examining matters is [a means of] deliverance from deception. Decisiveness of judgement (*ra'y*) is [a means of] safety from negligence and remorse. Consideration and forethought (*fikra*) reveal (*yakshifān 'an*) prudence and sagacity. Consultation with the wise is [a means of] making one's soul trustworthy and one's insight powerful. Ponder, therefore, before deciding; deliberate before forging ahead; and take counsel before proceeding.'

Again, [al-Shāfiʿī] said: 'The virtues are four in number. The first is wisdom, the basis of which is contemplation; the second is abstinence, the basis of which lies in appetite (*shahwa*); the third is strength, the basis of which lies in anger; and the fourth is justice (*ʿadl*), the basis of which lies in moderating (*iʿtidāl*) the forces of the ego.'

Such, then, are the sayings of the learned regarding contemplation. Not one of them, however, has [even] begun to describe its true nature (*sharaʿa fī dhikr ḥaqīqatihā*), or to explain its modalities and lines of thought.

---

39 Muḥammad ibn Idrīs al-Shāfiʿī (150-205/767-820), jurist and theologian and founder of the Shāfiʿī *madhhab* or juridical school, was born in Gaza, Palestine, raised in Mecca, and educated there and in Medina. A saintly figure of exemplary piety and scrupulousness, al-Shāfiʿī is also widely considered one of the greatest intellectual geniuses of Islam.

40 According to the Dār al-Minhāj edition of the *Iḥyā'*, this dictum is cited by Ibn al-Jawzī in *Ṣifat al-ṣafwa*, vol. 1/2, p. 151.

3

An exposition of the true nature and fruits of contemplation

KNOW that the meaning of 'contemplation' (*fikr*) is to bring together in the heart two cognitions (*maʿrifatayn*) in order to produce from them a third cognition. Take, for example, the case of a person who is inclined to [prefer] transitory things (*al-ʿājila*) and [so] goes in pursuit of the life of this lower world. Suppose that he [then] wishes to ascertain that the Next World is more deserving of preference than the lower world. There are two means by which he may do so. Firstly, he may be told by somebody else that the Afterlife is to be preferred to this life, and then adopt that opinion without himself gaining any insight into the essence of the matter (*ḥaqīqat al-amr*); and so he then inclines towards acting in a way that bespeaks preferring the Next Life to the life of this world, relying simply upon the word of the other person. That is called 'imitative acceptance' (*taqlīd*). It cannot be called 'direct knowledge' (*maʿrifa*). The second means consists of taking cognisance firstly of the fact that that which is more lasting is more worthy of preference, and then that the Afterlife is more lasting. One then derives from these two cognitions a third cognition: namely, that the Afterlife is more worthy of preference. That realisation can only be obtained by means of the two cognitions referred to. The process of making the heart aware of the two foregoing cognitions in order to arrive at a third cognition is termed either 'contemplation' (*tafakkur*), 'taking cognisance' (*i'tibār*), 'remembrance' (*tadhakkur*), 'consideration' (*naẓar*), 'reflection' (*ta'ammul*), or 'pondering' (*tadabbur*).

As regards the terms 'pondering', 'reflection', and 'contemplation', they are equivalent and express one and the same concept without any underlying variation of meaning. 'Recollection', 'taking note', and 'consideration', however, have divergent meanings even though what they designate is basically one and the same. The terms 'recollection', 'reflection', and 'consideration' differ in significance even though they share a single basic meaning. In the same way, the nouns *ṣārim*, *muhannad*, and *sayf* all refer to one [and the same] thing, but in different ways. *Ṣārim* ('trenchant [weapon]') denotes a sword inasmuch as it is sharp; *muhannad* ('[sabre] made from Indian [steel]') does so in relation to a place [of origin]; and *sayf* ('sword') does so in a manner not qualified by any allusion to such externals. Similarly, 'taking cognisance' (*i'tibār*) suggests the idea of bringing to mind two [distinct] cognitions in such a way as to progress from those two cognitions to a third. If that transition does not come about and the only possibility is to stop short at the two cognitions then one should use the term 'recollection', not 'taking cognisance'.

'Consideration' (*naẓar*) and 'contemplation' (*tafakkur*) are practiced when a third cognition is sought. One who does not seek a third cognition cannot be termed a 'considerer' (*nāẓir*). Again, while every 'contemplator' (*mutafakkir*) is a 'recollector' (*mutadhakkir*), not every 'recollector' is a 'contemplator'. The benefit of 'contemplative remembrance' (*tidhkār*) lies in the repetition of cognitions for the heart in order to establish them firmly and prevent their erasure from the heart. The benefit of contemplation lies in increasing one's knowledge and acquiring a cognition which hitherto was not available (*laysat ḥāṣila*). That is the difference between remembrance and contemplation.

When cognitions are brought together within the heart and are connected together in a particular order, they bear fruit in the form of further cognitions. So each cognition is the product of another cognition: when one cognition is obtained and links up with another, yet another cognition is produced in consequence. In this way the resultant [cognitions], insights and reflections [potentially] expand indefinitely, the process of augmenting one's cognitions being halted only by death or by hindrances of some kind.

All this applies to those who are capable of deriving benefit from [acquired] knowledge (*ʿulūm*) and are guided to the way of contemplation. Most people, however, are impeded from increasing their knowledge because they lack the [essential] capital resource, namely the cognitions by means of which one may make use of knowledge. [They are] like a person who has no goods and so is unable to make any profit; or like someone who has some goods but has no ability in trading and consequently gains nothing [from it]. In such cases [a person] has with him the cognitions which are the capital resource of knowledge but is no good at using it, bringing it together, or arranging the deals which lead to profitable trading.

In some cases, knowing how to utilise and derive benefit from [knowledge] springs from a Divine Light in the heart, one which arises from primordial human perfection (*fiṭra*). Such is the case with the Prophets – God's blessings be upon them all; but that is something rare indeed. [Alternatively], it may arise from self-training and practice; and this is the most common way. It can also happen that such cognitions arise in one who contemplates and that he reaps the fruits of them, but without being aware of how he did so and without being able to express them (*taʿbīr*), owing to his lack of experience in the art of expressing and adducing them [in argument] (*al-taʿbīr fī l-radd*).

How many men there are who know with true knowledge that the Afterlife is more worthy of preference but who, if asked as to the reason for their cognition of the fact, would be incapable of expressing or explaining it, even though it is nothing other than the conclusion drawn from two preceding cognitions, [which] were: that what is more lasting deserves preference, and that the Next World is more lasting than this world. From those cognitions they derive a third, namely that the Next World is more worthy of preference. In short, the essence of contemplation consists in bringing two cognitions to mind in order to arrive thereby at a third one.

As for the fruits of contemplation, they consist of knowledges, states, and actions. The fruit specific to each, however, is nothing other than a form of knowledge. When knowledge is acquired within the heart, the state of the heart is altered. When the heart's state changes, the actions of the bodily members change. Thus action follows state; state follows knowledge; and knowledge follows contemplation. Therefore contemplation is the beginning of, and the key to, all good.

What we have said thus far will show you how excellent a thing is contemplation (*tafakkur*) and how it surpasses invocation (*dhikr*) and remembrance (*tadhakkur*). For reflection (*fikr*) is *dhikr* with something else added. Remembrance with the heart is more meritorious than any physical action: the distinction (*sharaf*) of any action pertains to the *dhikr* within it. Consequently, contemplation is better than any other deed, for which reason it has been affirmed that 'One hour of contemplation is better than a year of worship.'[1] It is said also that it is [contemplation] which draws one away from reprehensible things to desirable ones, and from appetite and greed to abstinence (*zuhd*) and contentment. Again, it has been said that contemplation engenders direct witnessing and consciousness of Him (*taqwā*), for which reason He has said, Exalted is He, '*that they may become God-conscious or it may make them take heed.*'[2]

Should you wish to understand how contemplation transforms one's state, then take for example what was stated earlier about the Next Life, given that contemplation upon it brings us the knowledge that the Afterlife is preferable [to the life of this world]. Once such knowledge is firmly rooted in our hearts as a matter of certainty, our hearts change, turning towards desire for the Afterlife and renunciation of worldly things. That is exactly what we mean by 'state'.

Before this knowledge [is attained], the state of the heart is love for the transitory life and inclination towards it. With the knowledge in question, the state of the heart changes and its will and desire are altered. Moreover, the change of will yields as its fruit such actions of the body as involve repudiation of worldly things and dedication to works performed with the Next Life in view.

In this connection, five separate stages can be distinguished. First: remembrance (*tadhakkur*), which consists in bringing [to

---

1 A Tradition found in Ibn Ḥibbān, *Kitab al-'Aẓama*, as related by Abū Hurayra, with 'sixty years' in place of 'one year'; in Abū Manṣūr al-Daylamī's *Masnad al-Firdaws*, as related by Anas, with 'eighty years'; and in Abū al-Shaykh, from Ibn 'Abbās, with the wording 'better than a night's standing [in worship]'.

2 Qur'ān 20:113.

mind] two cognitions. Second: contemplation (*tafakkur*), which is the search for the cognition which one seeks to obtain from the two [already in mind]. Third: obtaining the desired cognition, and the heart's illumination by it. Fourth: a change in the heart from its former state, by virtue of the illumination gained. Fifth: the service performed for the heart by the bodily members in conformity with the new state prevailing within it.

When a stone is struck by a piece of iron, [a spark of] fire comes from it, illuminating the place [around it] and enabling the eyes to see around whereas previously they could not see; the limbs of the body are then brought into motion. In the same way, the tinderbox [that kindles] the light of cognition is contemplation (*fikr*). It combines two cognitions, just as stone and iron are brought together, joining them in a particular way just as a stone is struck against iron in a particular way. Thanks to this light, the heart is transformed so that it inclines towards something to which it did not before – just as one's ability to see is transformed by the light from the fire so that it can see what it could not see before. Thereupon one's limbs are aroused to action in accordance with the exigency of the state of his heart, in the same way that someone unable to act because of the [surrounding] darkness is aroused to action by being able to perceive with his sight what he could not see before.

The fruit of contemplation, then, consists of cognitions and of [spiritual] states. There is [potentially] no end to the cognitions; and the number of conceivable states affecting the heart is beyond the bounds of enumeration. Consequently, if an aspirant to the spiritual path (*murīd*) wished [fully] to enumerate the diverse branches of contemplation and the [possible] courses [they might follow], and [to determine] what he might reflect upon, he could not do so. The possible lines of contemplation are innumerable and their fruits limitless; but we shall attempt to provide some account of the [desirable] lines [of contemplation] and, in relation to them, of the most important aspects of the religious sciences as well as the states which form the way-stations of [spiritual] travellers.

This, however, will be no more than a summary account. A full exposition would entail an exposition of all the branches of knowledge; but these chapters [of the *Iḥyāʾ* taken] as a whole are like a commentary upon some of the sciences, in that they contain aspects of knowledge acquired by means of specific reflections. Let us proceed, therefore, to indicate the points which they have in common, so as to gain an awareness of the [diverse possible] directions that contemplation may follow.

4

Means and subjects for contemplation

KNOW that contemplation may involve some matter connected with religion, or matters unconnected with it. Our purpose is confined to religious subjects, and so we shall leave the other category aside. By 'religion' we mean the interaction (*muʿāmala*) that obtains between the servant and the Lord, Exalted is He.

All thoughts that can possibly occur to a servant [of God] relate either to the human being, his attributes, or his states; or else to the One Who is [to be] Worshipped (*al-Maʿbūd*), His Attributes, or His Actions. There can be no thought that does not fall into one of these two categories. Thoughts relating to the human may be concerned either with what is dear to the Lord, Exalted is He, or with what is displeasing [to Him]. There is no need to think of any matters outside these two categories. Thoughts relating to the Lord Most High may concern either His Essence, His Attributes, and His Most Beautiful Names, or else His Actions, His Sensory Domain (*Mulk*), His Spiritual Domain (*Malakūt*), and all that exists in the Heavens, the Earth, and what lies between them.

That the scope of contemplation [on matters pertaining to religion] is confined to the categories enumerated above will become evident to you if you consider [the following] simile. The state of those engaged in journeying towards God, Exalted is He, and of those who long to meet Him, can be likened to the state of those who are in love.

Let us take for example a person who is infatuated (*mustaḥtir*):

a lover whose attention is totally absorbed by his passion. He can think of nothing beyond what has to do with his beloved or himself. When thinking about his beloved he may reflect either on her loveliness and the beauty of her appearance in itself (*fī dhātih*), doing so in order to delight in thinking of her or gazing at her [with his mind's eye]; or alternatively he may reflect on the graceful and goodly actions that reveal her character and her qualities, so that this may double his pleasure and strengthen his love. While he is thinking about himself, his thoughts dwell upon those of his own characteristics which lower him in the sight of the one he loves, with a view to ridding himself of them; or upon those characteristics which bring him closer to her and endear him to her, with a view to acquiring them.

Should [the lover's] thoughts turn to any matter outside these two [general] categories, that contravenes the boundaries imposed by passionate love and constitutes a shortcoming therein. For a love that is complete and perfect is one that wholly engulfs the lover and fills the heart so entirely that no space remains in it for anything besides.

He who loves God, Exalted is He, should be the same. Neither his sight nor his contemplation should be directed to anything but his Beloved; whatever be the subject of his contemplation, if confined to the four categories [discussed above] it will certainly not contravene the exigencies of true love.

First category: reflection upon human qualities

Let us begin with the first category, namely reflection upon oneself and one's actions in order to distinguish between those that are liked and those that are disliked [by God]. It is this type of contemplation which pertains to the science of practical religion (*'ilm al-mu'āmala*), which in fact constitutes the object of this book.[1] The other category pertains to the science of intuitive unveiling (*'ilm al-mukāshafa*).

All things disliked by God or pleasing to Him can be classified

---

1 Meaning *Iḥyā' 'ulūm al-dīn* as a whole.

either as external, such as acts of obedience or disobedience [to Him], or as internal, such as those which lead to salvation or perdition. The latter, which are located in the heart, were discussed in detail [earlier in the *Iḥyāʾ*], in the Quarter on the Causes of Perdition (*Rubʿ al-Muhlikāt*) and the Quarter on the Means of Salvation (*Rubʿ al-Munjiyyāt*). Acts of obedience or of disobedience are divided into those concerned with [one of] the seven members and those concerned with the entire body, examples of the latter being deserting from the battle line, disobeying one's parents, or living in a forbidden dwelling.

For each of the things that are detested, it is necessary to reflect on three questions: [firstly,] whether or not it [really] is detested by God – which is not always obvious but which one may come to realise through careful consideration; [secondly,] if it is detested, one must study what are the means of safeguarding oneself from it; and [thirdly,] if one is currently given to that thing and so is obliged to give it up, whether one will be exposed to it in the future and consequently must take due precautions against it, or whether one has committed that thing in some situation in the past and hence is obliged to make amends for it. The same [or rather, analogous] categories apply to each of the things that are pleasing to God.

If we add together all the subjects outlined above, the possible lines of contemplation concerned with them number more than one hundred; and one will be led to contemplate all or most of them. To expound each of these subjects would be a lengthy business. The categories in question, however, are limited to four kinds: acts of obedience [to God]; acts of disobedience; the qualities that lead to perdition; and the qualities that lead to salvation. For each type we shall present one example so that the aspirant may judge the remainder by analogy, thus opening to him the gate of contemplation and broadening for him the way to it.

First Type: Acts of Disobedience [to God]

Every morning one should scrutinise in detail all seven members of the body, and then the body as a whole, in order to establish whether he is at that moment involved in committing some act of disobedience, from which he must therefore desist; or whether he has committed one the day before, in which case he must deal with it by desisting from and repenting of it; or whether he is bound to be exposed to [the danger of committing] it during the [coming] day, in which case he will prepare to guard himself against and keep well away from it. In the same way, one should scrutinise [the actions of] the tongue and declare that it will turn away from slander, lying, self-justification (*tazkiyat al-nafs*), ridiculing other people, expressing doubts (*mumārāt*), frivolous exchanges (*mumāzaḥa*), getting involved in what is none of one's business, and so on, and other such reprehensible acts.

One will begin, then, by acknowledging that those are actions that are detestable in the sight of God, Exalted is He, and will reflect upon the definitive statements (*shawāhid*) in the Qur'ān and Sunna regarding the terrible penalty incurred by [doing] them.

He will next reflect on how it is that he, in the situations [that life presents], is exposed to such promptings without being cognisant of the fact. In this way he will think about how he must safeguard himself against this. He must be aware that he will not be able to do so except either by [living in] seclusion and solitude (*infirād*), or else by keeping company with a righteous and godly man who will reproach him every time that he says something that is detestable to God. Failing that, if he sits with someone else [whose company is not so beneficial], let him put a stone in his mouth to serve him as a reminder. Such are the means by which one should consider the [appropriate] strategy by which to guard against [unlawful acts of the tongue].

One will [also] reflect on the faculty of hearing. He must pay no attention to backbiting, lying, vain and irrelevant talk, or frivolity or innovation [in religious matters]. [One must bear in mind that] such things he will hear only from Zayd and from 'Amr,[2] and that it behoves him to be on his guard against [such an individual], either by avoiding him or by the practice of forbidding what is wrong.

Whenever an act of disobedience concerns the stomach one

2 In Arabic the names Zayd and 'Amr stand for 'A' and 'B' in contexts such as this, and especially for two opposing parties in *fatwā*s and theoretical legal cases.

must consider whether, by filling it, he may not be disobeying God Most High in the matter of eating and drinking, whether it be by eating [too] much of what is lawful – for that is something which is detestable in the sight of God and which strengthens the appetites, the weapon of the Devil, God's enemy – or else by consuming that which is unlawful or suspect.

One should therefore examine the sources from which one's food and clothing are acquired, as well as one's housing and livelihood, and what are one's means of earning. He should also ponder on the ways and means to [obtaining] what is lawful. Next he must consider the right strategy to earn by such means and keep himself safe from anything unlawful. [A Muslim] ought to remind himself repeatedly that all his acts of worship will be lost [as invalid] by consumption of what is unlawful; that consuming [only] the lawful is the [very] foundation of all acts of worship; and that God Most High does not accept the ritual prayer of any bondsman the price of whose clothing includes a single dirham unlawfully acquired, as [Prophetic] Tradition relates.

In the same way one should reflect on [all] the members of one's body. What we have already said is sufficient without examining [the subject further] in detail. But whatever points one comes truly to know of these [blameworthy] states by means of contemplation, the bondsman must engage in constant vigilance (*murāqaba*) all day long in order to protect the members of his body from them.[3]

Second Type: Acts of Obedience [to God]

One should first examine how he performs those acts [of worship] prescribed for him as obligatory, and how to keep them free of shortcomings or defects, or how to make amends for defects by means of abundant supererogatory acts (*nawāfil*). After that, he should

3 On this subject see further the preceding Book (Book 38), *Kitāb al-Murāqaba wa l-Muḥāsaba* ('Vigilance and Calling Oneself to Account'). There is an annotated English translation by Anthony F. Shaker: *Al-Ghazālī on Vigilance and Self-Examination:* Kitāb al-murāqaba wa 'l-muḥāsaba, *Book XXXVIII of The Revival of the Religious Sciences* (Cambridge, 2015).

review his bodily organs one by one, and reflect on those actions pertaining to each of them which are dear to God, Exalted is He.

One may say, for example: 'The eye was created to contemplate '*the Realm of the Heavens and the Earth*',[4] and to derive lessons from them; also, to be employed in [acts of] obedience to God Most High; and to contemplate the Book of God, Mighty and Majestic is He, and the *Sunna* of His Emissary, may God exalt and preserve him. I am capable of occupying my eyes with studying the Qur'ān and the Sunna, so why am I not doing so? I am capable of looking with admiring eyes at So-and-so, who is obedient [to God], thus bringing joy to his heart, or of looking with contemptuous eyes at So-and-so, who is ungodly, thus restraining him from disobeying God; so why do I not do so?'

Likewise, one may declare, with reference to one's eyesight: 'I am capable of listening to the talk of someone who is troubled, or of listening to [words of wisdom] or knowledge, or of listening to recitation [of Qur'ān) or to remembrance [of God]. What is wrong with me, then, that I allow [my hearing] to be idle when God has bestowed it upon me and entrusted it to me so that I might give thanks to Him? What is wrong with me, then, that I deny the bounty given me therein by God, wasting it or letting it be idle?'

In the same way one should reflect upon the tongue and say, 'I am capable of drawing closer to God Most High by teaching, admonishing, expressing affection for the hearts of righteous people (*ahl al-ṣalāḥ*), by asking after the poor and bringing joy to the heart of Zayd the good and 'Amr the learned by means of some pleasant words. For any goodly word is [an act of] charity.'

Likewise, again, one should reflect on one's wealth (*māl*) and declare: 'I am capable of giving such-and-such an asset, for I can do without it. If ever I should find myself in need of it, God, Exalted is He, will provide the like of it for me. Should I need it at this moment, then I am intent upon the reward for giving preference to one who needs it more than I do.'

In the same way, one should scrutinise all his limbs, the whole of his body, and all his property – and, indeed, his animals, his servant boys, and his children. For all these things make up his

4 Qur'ān 6:75 and 7:185.

instruments and his worldly means, whereby he is capable of [acts of] obedience to God, Exalted is He. One should therefore work out through careful reflection which forms of pious obedience are feasible for him thanks to [these assets], and think about them with an eager desire to perform immense numbers of those pious acts.

[Again,] one must reflect on [the importance of] sincerity of intention in [carrying out] such acts, seeking the most likely place or time (*mazan*) [to find] the deserving, so that through them he may validate and purify his action and proceed with the rest of his acts of pious obedience in the same spirit.

Third Type: Qualities which lead to Perdition, these being located in the Heart

These [qualities] can be known from what we have mentioned in the Quarter concerning Matters which lead to Perdition. They consist of the seizure [of the soul] by lust, anger, avarice, arrogance, conceit (*ʿujb*), ostentation, envy, thinking ill, heedlessness, self-delusion, and other [vices].

[It is essential], then, to search one's heart for these qualities. Should one consider his heart to be entirely free (*munazzah*) from them, one must then reflect upon the nature of his [forthcoming] Trial and the bringing of testimony in the form of signs visible upon him. For the self is forever ready to make a favourable case for itself, and [forever] arguing. So when it claims to be humble and free from arrogance, one ought to put it to the test by carrying a bundle of firewood in the market, just as men of earlier times used to put their souls to the test by doing so. If [the self] claims to be forbearing, one should resist the anger that one feels towards another person, and then test one's ability to 'suppress rage.'[5] [One should also do] the same in regard to the remainder of the [evil] qualities [mentioned above].

This is reflection on the question as to whether or not one is characterised by detestable qualities. [Their presence] is indicated

5 An allusion to Qur'ān 3:134.

by the signs which we have mentioned in the Quarter concerning Matters which lead to Perdition. If there is a sign that indicates the presence of [any of] them, one must consider by what means those qualities can be made ugly in his own sight, and it can be made clear that they arise from ignorance, heedlessness, and the defilement of [satanic] intervention.

So then if one were to discern in one's ego conceit (*'ujb*) on account of some action he should reflect [on that] and say [to himself]: 'My action [was performed] only by means of my body, my limbs, my strength and my willpower. Yet all that is not [truly] from me or for me: it is purely something of God's making, and of His generosity to me. For it is He who created me, created my limbs, and created my strength and my willpower; it is He who by His Power caused my limbs to move; and the same applies to my strength and my willpower. How, then, could I feel conceit on account of an action or of my self, when I cannot fend for myself by myself (*lā qawām li-nafsī bi-nafsī*)?'

[Again], if one were to sense arrogance (*kibr*) in one's ego, one should remind himself of the stupidity in the ego, and tell it: 'Why do you see yourself as greater [than others], when the [truly] great one is he who is great in the sight of God? That is something that will be revealed after death. How many who at present are unbelievers will die as people near to God, and how many [who are now] Muslim will die condemned to Hell (*shaqiyyan*) because of a change of state, coming to a bad end [to their destinies] (*sū' al-khātima*)!' So once one has recognized that arrogance leads to perdition and that its original cause is stupidity, he should reflect on the remedy by which to eliminate that [fault] by practicing the actions of the humble.[6]

If one finds in one's ego a lust and an inordinate appetite for food, one should reflect on the fact that this is a characteristic of four-footed beasts (*bahā'im*), and that were there any perfection in the lust for food or for sexual intercourse then that would assuredly have been one of the Attributes of God and the qualities of the

---

6 For a detailed treatment of *'ujb* and *kibr*, see *Al-Ghazālī on Condemnation of Pride and Self-Admiration* (Kitāb dhamm al-kibr wa'l-ujb), *Book XXIX of The Revival of the Religious Sciences*, tr. Mohammed Rustom (Cambridge, 2018).

angels, as are knowledge and determinative power (*qudra*), which characteristics are not possessed by animals. The stronger that lust of his, the more he resembles the four-footed beasts and is far removed from the angels and from those brought nigh [to God]. One should also repeat [a similar exercise] with one's ego in regard to anger and then reflect on the [appropriate] method of effecting a cure.

The whole of this subject we have discussed in these chapters [of the *Iḥyā'*]; and therefore anyone wishing to extend his [methodical] practice of contemplation cannot dispense with studying the contents of those chapters.[7]

Fourth Type: Saving Qualities

This category [comprises] repentance, remorse for sins [committed], patient endurance of trials, thankfulness for blessings [received], fear, hope, detachment from this world, wholeheartedness, sincerity in acts of obedience [to God], love and reverence for God, being well pleased with [all] He does, ardent desire for Him, submissiveness, and humility. We have dealt with all those matters in this Quarter [the last Quarter of the *Iḥyā'*, on Saving Qualities], mentioning [both] the means of [obtaining] them and their [distinguishing] marks. The servant [of God] should therefore consider in his heart each day which of these qualities may give him protection, being qualities which bring one closer to God Most High. Then when he acknowledges that he is in need of any one of them he must be aware that [those saving qualities] are states of being which can only bear fruit through [branches of] knowledge, and that [branches of] knowledge can only bear fruit through reflections.

Consequently, if he wants to acquire for himself a state of

7 To what the author has said in this section about the factors which may prevent the aspiring traveller from progressing spiritually, one may perhaps add this warning, from elsewhere in the *Iḥyā'*: 'An aspirant who has devoted himself to remembrance and meditation [*fikr*] may be divided' (*sic*, i.e. diverted) 'from the Path by many things, such as self-satisfaction, ostentation, or joy at the states which are unveiled to him, and at the initial charismata…' See *Al-Ghazālī on Disciplining the Soul & On Breaking the Two Desires: Books XXII and XXIII of The Revival of the Religious Sciences*, tr. T.J. Winter (Cambridge, 1997), p. 97.

repentance and remorse, he should firstly scrutinise his sins and reflect upon them; he should collect them [as a case] against his soul and regard them in his heart as being immense. One should then consider the threat [of punishment] and severity [of chastisement] for them as laid down by the Sacred Law, and realise in one's soul the truth that he faces the wrath of God Most High, in order to provoke in it a state of remorse.

If one wishes to induce in one's heart a state of thankfulness, he should contemplate God's generosity (*iḥsān*) towards him, the forms of support He gives him, and how He extends to him His comely veiling [of sins] (*jamīl sitrih*). [He must do so] in the way that we expounded in part in the Book of Gratitude;[8] and so one should study that.

If one wishes [to acquire] a state of love and yearning, he should contemplate God's Majesty and Beauty, His Might (*ʿaẓama*) and His Exaltedness (*kibriyāʾ*). That [can be achieved] by contemplating the wonders of His Wisdom and the extraordinary features (*badāʾiʿ*) of His Creative Power. We shall be alluding to part of these in [our discussion of] the second category of contemplation.

If one wishes [to acquire] a state of fear, let him contemplate first his sins, outward and inward; then death and its attendant agonies. After that, he should contemplate what comes after death: the Questioning by Munkar and Nakīr,[9] the Torment in the grave, with its snakes, scorpions and worms; then the terror of the Summons at the Sounding of the Trumpet [for Resurrection]; then the terror of the Mustering [for Judgement] as all creatures are assembled on an equal footing; then the disputations of the Reckoning; then the Distress of [accounting for] every minute matter down to the spot or pellicule of a date-stone; then the Traverse,[10] its narrowness and sharpness; then his Moment of Truth, when he shall be turned to the left and be one of the Companions of Hell-Fire or turned to

8 Book 32 of the *Iḥyāʾ*. See *Al-Ghazālī on Patience and Thankfulness*, Kitāb al-Ṣabr wa al-Shukr: *Book XXXII of* The Revival of the Religious Sciences, tr. H.T. Littlejohn (Cambridge, 2010).

9 Munkar and Nakīr: the fearsome angels who interrogate the dead soon after their burial.

10 Al-Ṣirāṭ, the narrow and perilous bridge over which all must safely cross in order to reach the safety of Paradise.

the right and be given to dwell in the Home of [Eternal] Abiding. After the terrors of the Resurrection he should then picture in his heart the form of Hell, with its descending stairways, its obstacles, its horrors, its chains, fetters, Zaqqūm trees,[11] and pus, the diverse torments [found] in it; the ugliness of the outer forms of the Zabāniya,[12] its overseers; and how each time the skins [of the damned] are thoroughly cooked they change them for other skins;[13] how whenever [the damned] want to escape from [Hell] they are brought back to it;[14] and how when they see it from afar they hear its angry seething and sighing.[15] Likewise, one should go over all that is mentioned in the Qur'ān by way of descriptions [of Hell].[16]

If one wishes to summon up a state of hope, he should contemplate Paradise, its tranquil bliss, its trees, its rivers, its houris, its youths, its endless delight, and its everlasting kingdom.

Such is the method of contemplation whereby one should seek the kinds of knowledge which give rise to the inducing of states beloved [to God] or to the avoidance of objectionable characteristics. We have already discussed each of those states in individual chapters, to which one may refer for help in the details of their contemplation. But as regards recollection of these states as a whole, no more profitable [exercise] exists than reading of the Qur'ān with reflection, for that embraces every spiritual station and state and in it there is healing for all creation; and it contains that which confers fear, hope, patience, thankfulness, love, yearning, and all other [praiseworthy] states. It also contains that which keeps one away from all reprehensible states. It is therefore befitting that the servant [of God] recite it, repeating time and again the verse upon which he needs to reflect, even if it be a hundred times. To read a single verse with reflection and understanding is better than reading [the

11 Zaqqūm: the thorn-trees of Hell, which torment the damned. See Qur'ān 37:62, 44:43, 56:52.

12 Al-Zabāniya: the fierce angels in charge of Hell. See Qur'ān 96:18.

13 See Qur'ān 4:56.

14 See Qur'ān 32:20.

15 See Qur'ān 25:12 and 67:7-8.

16 See also, on the practice of reflection upon death, the Last Day, and the Afterlife, *The Remembrance of Death and the Afterlife* (Kitāb dhikr al-mawt wa-mā ba'dahu, *Book XL of* The Revival of the Religious Sciences (Iḥyā' 'ulūm al-dīn), tr. T.J. Winter (Cambridge, 1989).

Qur'ān] from cover to cover without pondering or understanding it. One should pause for reflection, even if it takes a [whole] night. Beneath every word [of every verse] lie innumerable secrets, of which one can only become aware through painstaking thought, together with a purity of heart [achievable only] after [practicing] sincere conduct [in relation to God].

The same [applies to] the study of the Traditions of the Emissary of God, may God exalt and preserve him, since he was endowed with comprehensive perfections of concise speech (*jawāmi' al-kalim*), and every word that he uttered represents an ocean of wisdom. If a true man of knowledge were to reflect upon it as it deserves, he would [be obliged to] look into it uninterruptedly for the whole of his lifespan.

The exposition [even] of individual verses or Traditions is a lengthy matter (*yaṭūl*). Look [for example] at [the following] saying of [the Prophet], may God bless and preserve him. 'The Spirit of Holiness [Gabriel] inspired these words in my soul: "Love whom you will, you shall part from them; live as you wish, you shall die; do as you wish, you shall be requited for it."'[17] Truly these words combine the wise sayings (*ḥikam*) of the men of ancient and modern times. They could suffice for a lifetime anyone reflecting upon them; were [such people] to pause [to consider at length] their inner meaning so that [the words] imposed themselves upon their hearts with the force of certainty, [those meanings] would surely absorb them entirely and that [condition] would intervene to preclude their paying any attention whatever to this world.

Such, then, is the method by which to reflect upon the branches of knowledge concerned with interaction [with God] (*'ulūm al-mu'āmala*) and the qualities of character of the servant, with regard to whether they are [such as are] liked or disliked by God. For the beginner [on the spiritual path] it is befitting to be continually absorbed in such thoughts, in order that his heart may be imbued with praiseworthy traits and noble stations and that he may be purified both inwardly and outwardly of all things disliked [by God]; and that he may know that although this is better than any [other] act of worship it does

17 This Hadith is also cited by the author in Book 1, *Kitāb al-'Ilm* (Knowledge), and Book 34, *Kitāb al-Faqr wa al-Zuhd* (Poverty and Abstinence).

not represent the final objective [of the path]. In fact, anyone who is occupied with [this exercise] is veiled from the objective of the people of total sincerity (*al-ṣiddīqūn*), which is to enjoy the bliss of contemplating the Glory and the Beauty of God, Exalted is He, the heart being so far absorbed in Him that he is annihilated from himself. That is to say, he forgets his own self, states, stations and qualities so that his attention is wholly engrossed in the [Divine] Beloved. [He becomes] like an obsessive lover when he encounters the one whom he loves: unable for one instant to examine the state and characteristics of his own soul, he remains instead like a man utterly bemused and forgetful of himself. For those in love, this is the ultimate pleasure.

What we have been discussing is reflection concerned with the rectification of one's inner being so that it may be put in order with a view to drawing close and attaining [to God]. But if one were to waste one's entire life [only] in putting oneself in order, when would he enjoy the bliss of nearness [to God]? That is why [Ibrāhīm] al-Khawāṣṣ[18] used to wander around in the wastelands. When al-Ḥusayn ibn Manṣūr [al-Ḥallāj][19] met him, [al-Ḥallāj] asked him, 'What is your situation?' (*Fī mā anta*).] He replied, 'I am wandering in desert lands, rectifying my spiritual state of complete trust [in God] (*fī al-tawakkul*).' 'You have let your lifetime pass (*afnayta*) in rectifying your inner state,' said al-Ḥusayn [al-Ḥallāj]. 'Where is [your] extinction in the Supreme Unity (*al-fanā' fī al-tawḥīd*)?'

It is Extinction in [God] the Unique Truth which is the final goal of seekers and the ultimate bliss of those of perfect faith (*al-ṣiddīqūn*). The process of purifying oneself of those characteristics that lead to perdition, then, follows a course [analogous] to passing through a period of waiting (*'idda*) before [re-]marriage.[20] The acquisition of those characteristics that lead to salvation, and

18 Ibrāhīm al-Khawāṣṣ (d. 291/903), a great early Sufi, is known especially for his asceticism and his long periods of travel.

19 Al-Ḥusayn ibn Manṣūr al-Ḥallāj, the renowned and controversial Sufi of Baghdad, executed for heresy in 309/922.

20 Islamic sacred law (*sharī'a*) imposes a period of waiting after divorce or being widowed, during which a woman may not remarry. This is normally four months and ten days; for those too young or old to menstruate, it is three months; in the case of pregnancy it lasts until after childbirth. See Qur'ān 2: 234.

of other acts of obedience [to God], on the other hand, follows a course [analogous] to a woman preparing her trousseau, making up her face and combing her hair in order to be fittingly ready for the meeting with her bridegroom. If, however, she were to spend her entire lifetime in ascertaining that she is not pregnant and in beautifying her face, that would be a barrier to her [ever] meeting her beloved.

You must understand the way of things in religion in the same way, if you are of those who seek to sit in [God's] presence (*ahl al-mujālasa*). But if you are like a bad servant, who will only bestir himself from fear of a beating or desire for reward, then be warned (*fa-dūnak*) that you must tire your body with outward actions, for between you and your heart is a thick veil. Provided that you have fulfilled your duty in terms of actions, you will be one of the people of Paradise. But companionship (*mujālasa*) [with God] is for folk of a different kind (*aqwām ākharūn*).

Once you have become acquainted with the way in which to reflect upon the relationship between the servant and his Lord, you should adopt this as a custom and a practice [each] morning and evening. Thus you will not forget your self, those qualities of yours which keep you distant from God, Exalted is He, or the states you possess that bring you closer to Him, Glorified and Exalted is He. Indeed, every aspirant [to the Spiritual Path] ought to have a notebook in which he records all characteristics that are conducive to perdition, all characteristics conducive to salvation, all acts of disobedience, and all acts of obedience; and he should examine his soul for them every day.

As regards those that are conducive to perdition, it will suffice for him to look closely for ten of them, for if free of those he will be free of the others: stinginess, pride, conceit, hypocrisy, excessive anger, greed for food, sexual lust, love of wealth, and love of prestige. Ten of the saving qualities, too, [suffice for the purpose]: remorse for one's sins, endurance of trials, ready acceptance of the [Divine] decree, gratitude for bounties received, equilibrium between hope and fear, detachment from this world, sincerity in one's actions, [acting with] good character with people, love for God Most High, and total submission to Him. That makes twenty traits of character [in all]: ten blameworthy and ten praiseworthy. Whenever one has eliminated a blameworthy trait one should cross it off in the notebook and cease to reflect upon it, [instead] thanking God Most High for dealing with it on his behalf and for purifying one's heart of it. One should realize, too, that it could not have been accomplished but for the support and help of God, Exalted is He, and that had He left one to one's own devices one could never have been able to erase from one's soul the least of one's vices. One should then proceed to the nine remaining [bad traits] and do the same until one has crossed them all out.

In the same way, one should impose it upon oneself to acquire the [ten] characteristics conducive to salvation. When one has acquired one of them, such as repentance and remorse for example, one should cross it out and [then] occupy oneself with the remainder. This is required of the diligent novice; but for most of those of mankind who are numbered among the righteous it is appropriate that they record in their notebooks any manifest misdeeds, such as eating something [of] doubtful [legality] or loosening the tongue and committing backbiting, tale-bearing, ostentation, self-praise, going to excess in enmity towards enemies and friendship towards friends, or currying favour with people by failing to bid them do what is right and forbid them to do what is wrong. The majority of those who count themselves [as being] among the righteous are not unblemished by all these bodily acts of disobedience. Until the bodily actions are pure of sins, it is not possible to edify and purify the heart.

Each category of people being subject to some type of disobedience, their search and their contemplation must be directed towards that, rather than towards those they are free from. Take, for example, a scholar [who practices] scrupulous abstinence from what is legally doubtful. Such an individual will not, in most cases, be free from the desire to show off his knowledge, to court fame, and to extend his reputation through either his teaching or his preaching. Anyone who does so incurs an enormous danger, one that only those of perfect sincerity escape. For if his words are well received and make a good impression on people's hearts then he will not be devoid of conceit, vanity, pretence, and affectation;

and all these are causes of perdition. If, on the other hand, his words are rebutted then he will not be devoid of rage, disdain, and rancour towards the one who rebuts him, more than he would have towards one who rebutted the words of someone other than him. [Then] Satan may come to him in disguise and tell him, 'Your rage is due to their having refused and denied the truth.' But if he finds there to be a difference between [his reaction to] his own rebuttal and that of another learned person, then he is deluded and is the laughing-stock of Satan. Thereafter, for as long as he feels at ease with [popular] acceptance, he is delighted by praise, and he detests being rebutted or shunned, he will not be free of affectation and artificiality, refining his elocution (*lafẓ*) and his delivery (*īrād*), being avid to win praise; but God does not like those who are affected. And the Devil may come to him in disguise and say: 'Your avidity to refine your elocution, and your affectation in doing so, are only [intended] for disseminating the truth, and so that it may make a good impression in the heart, [all] to elevate the religion of God Most High.' Now, if his delight at his fine enunciation and in people praising him for it is greater than it would be if people were to praise one of his peers, then he has been duped and he is droning away (*yudandan*)[21] in pursuit of prestige among people even though he supposes his objective to be [aiding] the religion.

The more that his mind is pervaded by these traits, the more apparent that becomes in his outward [comportment], with the result that he becomes more respectful to those who revere him, being convinced of his superiority, and more pleased and delighted to meet with them, than with somebody who shows excessive friendship to someone other than him – even if that other person is deserving of that friendship. And it may be that for people of learning this ends up with them becoming jealous of one another the way that women do, and that it upsets him if one of his students spends time with another [scholar], even though he knows that he is benefiting from the other man and is profiting from him in his religion.

All of that [behaviour] is a subtle effect (*rashḥ*) of the destructive traits lurking in the inmost heart, from which a learned man may imagine himself to be safe when in fact he is deluded about them

21 Or, following an alternative reading, 'he is going about' (*yadūr*).

– and it is through these signs [just described] that this becomes apparent. Thus for scholars [of religion] the temptation (*fitna*) is enormous. He may be in control [of it], or he may be destroyed [by it]; and he has no prospect of the [way to spiritual] safety that ordinary people have. If any [religious scholar] perceives these traits in himself, it is imperative that he isolate himself, taking to seclusion and obscurity. If asked for a legal ruling he must resist [giving one]. In the time of the Companions, may God Most High be well pleased with them, the Mosque used to contain a number of Companions of the Envoy of God, may God exalt and preserve him, all of them qualified to give legal rulings; and yet they would all refer to each other to give a fatwa. Whichever of them [eventually] did so would have loved someone else to do so in his stead.

In this [situation], it behoves [such a scholar] to beware of Satanic humans saying: 'Don't do that [i.e. don't withdraw], because if that door were opened, [all of] the [religious] sciences would disappear among mankind!' Let him tell them, 'The faith of Islam has no need of me, for it was flourishing before my time and will likewise do so after it. Were I to die, the pillars of Islam would not be demolished. I, however, cannot dispense with rectifying my heart.' As for [the notion of] this entailing the disappearance of knowledge, that is an illusion that proves extreme ignorance. For [in fact] supposing people were to be imprisoned in a jail, shackled with bonds, and threatened with Hell-Fire if they should seek knowledge, [even then] the love of eminence and leadership would lead them to break their bonds, demolish fortress walls and escape them, and to engage in seeking knowledge. For [religious learning] will never vanish as long as Satan endears leadership to mankind; and Satan will never flag in his activity until the Day of Resurrection. He will incite to spreading knowledge groups of people who have no [destined good] share in the Afterlife. As the Emissary of God said, may God exalt and preserve him, 'God will support this religion by means of people who shall have no portion [of goodness Hereafter];'[22] and 'God will certainly aid this religion by means of immoral men.'[23] It is not fitting, therefore, for [such] a learned individual to be deluded by

22 Nasā'ī, *al-Sunan al-kubrā*, Hadith 8833.

23 Bukhārī, *Ṣaḥīḥ*, 3062; Muslim, *Ṣaḥīḥ*, Hadith 111.

these deceptive stratagems into mixing with people, thus fostering in his heart the love of position, praise, and being revered. That is the seed of [religious] hypocrisy. Said [the Emissary of God], may God exalt and preserve him, 'Love of rank and wealth causes hypocrisy to grow in the heart as water causes greenery to grow.'[24] He also said, may God exalt and preserve him, 'Ravening wolves let loose on a flock of sheep do not cause more damage to it than the love of rank and wealth cause to the religion of a Muslim man.'[25]

The love of prestige and wealth cannot be eradicated from the heart except by withdrawing from people, fleeing from associating with them, and giving up anything that might increase one's standing in their hearts. Let the learned man's thinking, therefore, be directed to making himself aware of the latent elements of these traits in his heart and finding a way to be rid of them. This is the duty of the godly scholar.

For the likes of us [laymen], however, it is fitting that our contemplation be [directed] upon that which will strengthen our belief in the Day of Reckoning, because if the righteous early [Muslims] saw us they would certainly say: 'These [people] do not [really] believe in the Day of Reckoning!' For our actions are not those of someone who believes in Paradise or Hell-Fire. Anyone who is afraid of something will flee from it, and anyone who is hoping for something will seek [to acquire] it. As we have already seen, the way to flee from Hell-Fire is to avoid anything doubtful or unlawful and refrain from acts of disobedience [to God], whereas we are engrossed in them. And the way to seek Paradise is to perform many voluntary acts of worship, whereas we fall short in performing [even] the obligatory ones. So it is that we gain as the fruits of knowledge nothing more than being led into greed for [the things of] this world and dogged pursuit of it. It is said that if this [worldliness] were something reprehensible then the learned would have more right to, and more aptitude in, avoiding it than we have. If only we were like ordinary laymen! When we died, our sins would die with us. How much more enormous, then, is the trouble we have exposed ourselves to, if we only thought [about

24 Hadith not found by al-'Irāqī.

25 Tirmidhī, *Sunan*, Hadith 2376; Ṭabarānī, *Awsaṭ*, Hadith 6275.

it]! So we ask God Most High to put us right and cause us to put things right, and to grant us enabling success in repenting before He takes our lives. Truly He is the Generous, the Kind One to us, the Liberal Bestower upon us.

These, then, are lines of reflection for the learned and the righteous regarding the knowledge of how to interact [with people] (*ʿilm al-muʿāmala*). Once they have [successfully] completed them, their attention [can] be diverted from themselves[26] and they may progress from that [concern] to contemplating the Majesty and Immensity of God and to enjoy beholding Him with the eye of the Heart. That can only be fully accomplished, however, after breaking free from all the qualities conducive to perdition and acquiring all those conducive to salvation. If something of that [contemplation of God] becomes manifest before that [purification is completed], it will be weak, defective, turbid, and subject to interruption. It will be fleeting like a lightning-flash, not stable or lasting. He will be like a lover who finds himself alone with his beloved, but beneath whose clothing are snakes and scorpions that sting him time after time. Thus his pleasure in beholding [God] will be disturbed and he will have no means of completing his enjoyment [of it] except to get the scorpions and snakes out of his clothing. These blameworthy qualities are scorpions, and they are harmful and disturbing; and in the grave the pain of the stinging [far] exceeds that of the stings of [ordinary] scorpions and snakes. Now, this is a sufficient amount of instruction about the ways in which to direct one's reflections upon those traits in one's soul which are dear to one's Lord, Exalted is He, and those which are detestable in His sight.

Second category: Reflection upon the Majesty, Might, and Glory of God

This comprises two stages (*maqāmān*). The highest [would be] to reflect upon His Entity (*dhāt*), His Attributes, and the meanings of His Names; but this is something that is forbidden, for the saying

26 Or, 'from their egos' (*ʿan anfusihim*).

goes 'Reflect upon the creating of Allah Most High, and not upon the Entity of Allah.'[27] This is because the mind is confounded in [the attempt to do so], for only people of perfected faith (*ṣiddīqūn*) are capable of turning their regard towards Him; and they lack the capacity to continue doing so. All other creatures, when they direct their sight towards the Majesty of God Most High, find themselves in the same position as a bat as regards the light of the sun. That animal cannot bear it at all, and so it hides itself in daytime and then arises in the evening, groping to find its way around as the last rays of light fall upon the Earth. The people of perfect faith, though, are like a man looking at the sun. He is capable of looking at it, but he cannot do so continually, for otherwise he would risk losing his eyesight; an eye [being] exposed to [direct] sunlight would cause discomfort to the eyes and damage one's eyesight. Likewise, to focus one's [mental] vision upon the Divine Entity leads to bewilderment (*ḥayra*), bafflement (*dahsh*), and mental disturbance.

The correct course, therefore, is not to approach the ways of reflection upon the Essence or the Attributes of God, Glorious is He, since the majority of minds are unable to withstand it. Instead [one should confine oneself to grasping] the small amount which one of the learned has explained, which is as follows. 'God Most High is Pure, Transcendent beyond location, spatial extent, or direction, being neither inside the world nor outside it, neither connected to the world nor separated from it.' This so confuses the minds of many kinds of people (*aqwām*) that they deny it, being unable to manage either to hear of it or to realise it. Indeed, there are those who cannot put up with even less than that. When they are told, 'He is Immense and Exalted above having a head, feet, hands, eyes, or limbs, and above having a body characterized by size or mass,' they reject this and suppose that notion to be derogatory to the Magnificence (*'aẓama*) and Majesty (*jalāl*) of God. In fact, one particularly stupid member of the general public has said, 'That is what an Indian watermelon is like, not what God is like!' – because the poor fellow supposes that majesty and might reside in those bodily members. This is because the [average] person only knows about himself, and considers only himself mighty. Consequently he

---

27 This saying is sometimes cited as a Hadith.

cannot comprehend the might that exists in anyone or anything with attributes that are unlike his own. Actually, the best he can manage (*ghāyatuh*) is to imagine himself as a handsome figure sitting on his throne, attended by page-boys who obey his [every] command. Inevitably, then, the best he can manage is to imagine the same of God, Exalted and Transcendent is He, in order to understand [the meaning of] magnificence. If a fly had a mind and if it were told, 'Your Creator does not have wings, arms or legs,' it would certainly deny that and it would reply, 'How could my Creator be more lacking than I am? Can He have had his wings cut off, or is He chronically ill and unable to fly? Can it be that I possess an organ and a faculty which He does not possess the like of, when He is my Creator, my Maker?' Most of mankind have minds that are close to being like that mind. Truly man is most ignorant, wrongdoing and ungrateful, for which reason God Most High revealed to one of His Prophets: 'Do not inform My servants of My Attributes, lest they deny Me; inform them about Me in a way they can understand.'

Since contemplating the Essence and Attributes of God, Exalted is He, is perilous, for the reasons just explained, the etiquette of Sacred Law and the best interests of people dictate that one should not direct the course of one's contemplation towards them. Instead, we will move on from that to the alternative viewpoint (*al-maqām al-thānī*), which is to consider His Actions, the ways of His Providence (*majārī qadarih*), the marvels of His Creative Power, and the wonders of His direction of His Creation (*badāʾiʿ amrih fī khalqih*). For they give proof of His Majesty, His Exalted Might (*kibriyā*), His Transcendent Perfection and Exaltedness; they are also proof of the perfection of His Knowledge and His Wisdom and the execution of His Will and His Omnipotent Power. His Attributes can be beheld in the effects of His Attributes, since we cannot withstand looking [directly] at His Attributes just as we cannot endure looking [directly] at the sun; and so we look at the earth however much it is illuminated by the sunlight. From this we infer the magnitude of the sun's light, as well as that of the light of the moon and the other heavenly bodies. The light of the Earth is one of the effects of the sun's light, and to look at an effect is to receive definitive guidance as to the cause of that effect even though it cannot take the place of looking at the cause itself. The totality of existent things in this world is one of the effects of the Omnipotent Power of God Most High, a light among the lights of His Being. Indeed, there is no darker darkness than [that of] non-existence, or light brighter than [that of] existence. The existence of all things is one of the Lights of His Being, Exalted and Transcendentally Perfect is He. For the fundamental support of the existence of things is through His Essence, the Eternally Subsistent through Himself, just as the basic support of the light of physical bodies is through the light of the sun, which radiates light by itself, whenever and wherever part of the sun is uncovered.

Now, the customary [way to look at sunlight] is to position a basin of water so that the sun can be seen [reflected] in it and one can look at it. Thus the water becomes the means of averting the eyes slightly from the sun's light in such a manner that one's eyesight can withstand it. Likewise, [divine] Actions are the medium whereby we can see the Attributes of the Actor; and the Light of the Essence will not dazzle us once we have distanced ourselves from it through the medium of the Actions. This is the secret of [the Prophet's] words, may God exalt and preserve him: 'Reflect upon God's creation, but do not reflect on the Essence of God Most High.'[28]

How to reflect upon what God Most High has created

Know that all that exists apart from God Most High represents God's Action and Creation; and every atom there is, be it substance or accident (*'araḍ*), quality (*ṣifa*) or qualified entity (*mawṣūf*), contains wonders and marvels in which God's Wisdom, Omnipotence, Majesty and Immensity are manifested. To enumerate [all of] that is not possible; but we shall point out some categories (*jumal*) of them to serve as examples of the rest of them. We say that created entities fall into the following categories.

[Firstly, there are] those whose origin (*aṣl*) is not known, and on which it is not possible to reflect. How many things there are in existence which we do not know! As God Most High has said,

28 See p. 7.

'*And He creates that which you know not*';[29] *Incomparably Glorious is He Who created all of the pairs: of that which the Earth grows, of yourselves, and of that which you do not know.*'[30] He has also said, Exalted is He, '*And for Us to bring you forth* [*again*] *in that which you know not*.'[31]

[Secondly, there are] those whose origin and general [nature] is known but whose details are not, but on the details of which it is [nevertheless] possible for us to reflect. These [in turn] are divided into those which we may perceive by means of eyesight and those which we cannot see. As for those which we cannot see with our eyes, such as the angels, the jinn, the devils, the [Divine] Footstool, the [Divine] Throne, etc., the scope for reflecting on those things is narrow and recondite (*yughmaḍ*). Let us, then, pass on from them to that which is closer to our power of understanding – that is to say, what is perceptible by eyesight: the seven heavens and the Earth, and that which lies between [the former and the latter].

The heavens can be observed in their stars, suns and moons, their movements and their turning in their risings and settings. The earth can be observed in what it contains by way of mountains, minerals, rivers and seas, animals and plants; and what is between the sky and the earth – that is, the air – in clouds, rainfall, icy precipitation, thunder, lightning, thunderbolts, shooting stars, and violent winds.

These are categories [of things] that can be witnessed in the heavens, in the earth, and between them. Each category can be divided into types; each type can be divided into sub-types; each sub-type branches out into classes; and there is no end to these ramifications and subdivisions in accordance with the diversity of [their] qualities, constitution (*hay'a*), and outward and inner significations (*ma'ānī*). All of that offers scope for contemplation. Not one atom moves in the heavens or the earth, be it inanimate, vegetable or animal, heavenly sphere or star, but that God Most High is its Mover. In its movement there may be [one aspect of] wisdom, or two, or ten, or a thousand! All of that is a witness to God Most High regarding [His] Unicity, and evidence of His Majesty and Sovereign Might;

29 Qur'ān 16:8.

30 Qur'ān 36:36.

31 Qur'ān 56:61.

and these are [also] signs that prove [the existence of] Him. The Qur'ān urges [mankind] to reflect upon these signs. As He has said, Exalted is He: *'Truly in the creation of the heavens and earth and the alternation of night and day are signs for those with insight'.*[32] He has also said, Exalted is He, [in passages] from the beginning of the Qur'ān to the end, *'Among His Signs is/are... .'*[33]

Signs of God in Man

One of His Signs is the human being, created from a sperm-drop. You are yourself the closest thing to you. Within you there are wonders proving the greatness of God Most High; so much so that it would take you an entire lifetime to study one hundredth part of them, though your mind still would not be capable of this. How negligent you are, to be so ignorant of yourself! How, then, could you aspire to know others? But God Most High has commanded you in His Noble Scripture to reflect upon yourself, saying *'And within yourselves* [*are signs*]*; can you not see?'*[34] He has reminded you that you were created from a sperm-drop, saying, *'Confound man! What an ingrate he is! From what did God create him? He created him and formed him from a drop of seed; then showed him the way; then caused him to die and be buried; then, when He wishes, He will restore him to life.'*[35] He also says, *'And one of His signs is that He created you from dust – and then there you are as humans, scattering far and wide'*;[36] and *'Was he not once a mere drop of ejaculated sperm, then a soft blood-clot which God created and formed?'*;[37] *'Did We not create you from a base*

---

32 Qur'ān 3:190.

33 This is not literally accurate in terms of the standard numerical order of Sūras in the Qur'ān. The first occurrences are in Sūra 30 (al-Rūm), *āyas* 20-21 and 46. The phrase is also found in two other Sūras: 41 (Fuṣṣilat), 37 and 39; and 42 (al-Shūrā), 29 and 32. In the Qur'ān, the word *āyātunā/āyātinā* (Our Signs) is used mainly to refer to Divine Revelation and/or to miraculous Signs of God); *āyātuhu/āyātihi* is used both for those and for more commonly observable or noted signs in creation.

34 Qur'ān 51:21.

35 Qur'ān 80:17-22.

36 Qur'ān 30:20.

37 Qur'ān 75:37-38.

fluid which We placed in a safe vessel until a fixed time?';[38] and again, '*We created mankind from a sperm-drop and mixed fluids.*'[39] He has then described how He made the sperm-drop into a blood-clot, the blood-clot into a lump, and [made] the lump bones, saying, Exalted is He: '*We created man from an extract of clay; then We made him a sperm-drop in a secure lodging-place; then We made the sperm-drop a blood-clot*' and so on, to the end of the verse.[40]

The [purpose of] the repeated mention of the sperm-drop in the Glorious Scripture is not for the word to be heard and reflection on its meaning disregarded. Now, consider the sperm-drop: it is a drop of dirty liquid which if left for a moment would be struck by the air, decay, and decompose. [Look at] how the Lord of Lords extracted it from the loins and thorax! [Consider] how He joined together male and female, implanted affection and love in their hearts, leading them on to intercourse by the chains of love and appetite; how He extracted the seed from the man through the movement of coition; how He drew menstrual blood from the depths of veins and collected it in the womb. After that, [consider how] He created a newborn [to be] from a sperm-drop, gave it menstrual fluid to drink, and nourished it so that it grew, increased [in size], and became sizeable; how He turned the sperm-drop, which was bright white, into a red blood-clot; and how He then turned the blood-clot into a lump. Next, [consider] how He divided the different parts of the sperm-drop, each being similar and equal, into bones, nerves, veins, sinews, and flesh; then, how He assembled the external members from pieces of flesh, nerves, and veins. He made the head rounded, piercing it with [the organs of] hearing and eyesight, the nose, the mouth, and the rest of the orifices. Next, He extended the arms and legs, dividing their extremities into fingers and toes and giving these tips with nails. Then [consider] how He assembled the internal organs – the heart, stomach, liver, spleen, lungs, womb, bladder, and intestines, every single one of which has a particular shape, size, and function. Then consider how He divided each of these limbs

38 Qur'ān 77:20-22.

39 Qur'ān 76:2.

40 Qur'ān 23:12-14. The remainder of verse 14 completes the outline description of the miracle of embryonic development.

and organs into parts. He assembled the eye in seven layers, each having a particular description and form. If one of those layers were missing, or any of those attributes ceased to be, the eye would be deprived of the power to see.

Were we to go on to describe the marvels and signs in each one of these limbs and organs, [whole] lifetimes would pass [in the meantime]. Now consider bones, which are strong and hard: how He created them from a simple, soft sperm-drop, then turned them into a structure and support for the [whole] body, then made them to measure in various shapes and sizes: some small and others large, some long and others round, some hollow and others solid, some wide and others narrow.

Since a human being needs to be capable of moving the entirety of his body or some of his limbs, and requires to come and go in [meeting] his needs, [God] did not make him a single bone but many bones with joints between them to make it easy for him to move about; He also made to measure the form of each of them in accordance with the [type and extent of] movement required of it. Next, He linked together their joints, connecting them with ligaments which He caused to grow at one end of [each] bone and fastened to the other end [of the adjoining bone] as the ligament for [securing] it. After that, He created at one end of the bone protrusions from it, and the other end a cavity within it to match the shape of the protrusions so that they could enter it and fit into it [precisely]. Thus it is that when a servant (of God) wishes to move a part of his body there is no impediment to him [doing so]. But were it not for the joints that would certainly have been hard for him, if not impossible (*la-taʿadhdhara ʿalayh*).

Furthermore, consider how [God] created the bones of the skull: how He made and assembled its components. He assembled it from fifty-five bones of varying shapes and forms, bringing them together in such a way that the rounded form of the head took shape as you see it. These [bones] comprise six belonging to the cranium, fourteen for the upper jaw (*ḥayy*), and two for the lower jaw. The remaining [bones] are the teeth, some of which are broad and suited to grinding and some sharp and suited to cutting; these are the canines, molars, and middle incisors.[41]

Next, [God] made the neck as the mounting for the head, fashioning it from seven round, hollow beads (*kharzāt*) in which are irregularities (*taḥrīfāt*), protrusions and gaps to connect them to one another. To describe the aspects of [Divine] wisdom in that would be a lengthy matter. He then assembled the neck upon the spine, composing the spine, [extending] between the base of the neck and the extremity of the pelvic bone, from twenty-four discs. He assembled the pelvis from three different parts and connected to the base of it the coccyx, which is also made of three parts. Next, He connected the backbones to the chest-bones, the shoulder-bones, the bones of the arms, the pubic bones, and the pelvis. After that, He put in place the thigh-bones and those of the lower leg and the feet. We will not prolong [this account] by discussing the numbers involved in all of that.

The total number of bones in the human body is two hundred and forty-eight,[42] not counting the small bones that fill the interstices of the joints. Consider, then, how [God] created the whole of that from one pitiful, delicate sperm-drop! The point of mentioning the number of bones is not so that we may know how many there are; that is readily accessible information which is known to physicians and anatomists. The objective is purely that we may [continue] from reflecting on them to [reflecting on] Him who planned and created them: how He made them to measure, planned them, made them in varying shapes and sizes, and made them a specific number. For had He added even one more, it would assuredly have been a bane for humanity requiring its removal; and had He left even one out, it would assuredly have been a defect requiring remedial treatment (*jabr*). Hence a physician ought to look into what treatment might be applied to remedy such a problem, and a person of insight should regard this [perfectness of the number of bones] as proof of the gloriousness of their Creator and Shaper. What a vast difference there is between those two perspectives!

---

41 Logically, the molars should come first; but this is how the text has it. According to modern medical science there are twenty-two bones in the skull.

42 Modern medicine reckons the number of bones in the human body at 206; the difference can be partly accounted for by the author counting the teeth as bones and by his count of the bones in the skull.

Next, consider how God Most High created the instruments for moving the bones, namely the muscles. He created in the human body five hundred and twenty-nine muscles. A muscle is composed of flesh and nerves, ligaments and coverings, varying in size and shape according to their location and the power they are required to have. Twenty-four of them control the movement of the pupil and lids of the eye; and if a single one of them were lacking, the operation of the eye would be vitiated. Likewise, every limb and organ has a specific number of muscles of specific size.

Even more wonderful than all of that is the design of the nerves, veins, and arteries and their number, sources, and ramification. To explain it would take too long, but there is scope for reflection on every single one of these [small] parts [of the body] and, furthermore, on every single one of these limbs; and, again, on the whole body.

The whole of that [which has just been said] was a consideration of the wonders of the body. However, the wonders of the hidden meanings and qualities which are inaccessible to the senses are greater. Now look at the outward and inward aspects of the human being, his body, and his [inner] attributes. You will see there enough marvels and workmanship to exhaust every possibility of marvelling. And all of that is the handiwork of God, Glorious and Majestic is He, [exercised] upon a droplet of dirty fluid! You [can] see, then, Whose handiwork that is within a [mere] droplet of fluid; what, then, of His handiwork in the realm of the heavens and the stars in them? What wisdom of His resides in their positions, forms, sizes, and numbers, in the conjunction of some and the disjunction of others, the variations in their [constellated] forms and the disparities between their places of rising and setting? For you must not suppose that there is a single particle in the realm of the heavens that is devoid of [Divine] Wisdom and manifestations of wisdom (*ḥikam*). On the contrary, they are more full of wisdom (or: stronger: *aḥkam*) in construction, [yet] more perfect in craftsmanship, and a [yet] vaster combination of wonders, than the human body. Indeed, there is no comparison (*nisba*) between all that the Earth contains and the wonders of the heavens. For this reason (God) has said, Exalted is He: '*Are you mightier in [your] creation, or the heaven? He constructed it, raised its vault, then formed it, covered over its night, and brought forth its forenoon brightness.'*[43]

Now go back to the sperm-drop and think about how it was at first, and what has happened to it secondly. Reflect on this: if all of mankind and the jinn combined together to create for the sperm-drop hearing, sight, intelligence, power, knowledge, or a spirit – or to create within it [one] bone, vein, nerve, [piece of] skin, or hair – would they be able to do so? Indeed, even if they [only] wished to know about its essential reality and the nature of its physiognomy (*khilqa*), after God Most High had created that, they would certainly be powerless to do so.

What is astounding about *you*, however, is this. If you were to look at a picture of a human being painted on a wall, to the drawing of which an artist had applied the maximum of skill so that it came close to the [actual] form of a human being – and if the spectator were to say, 'It is just as if it were a [real] person' – you would wonder at the artist's creativity, skill and manual dexterity and the perfection of his intelligence. There would be immense admiration of him in your heart, and that despite the fact that you are aware that that picture was only produced by means of paint, a pen, a wall, a hand, ability, knowledge, and will-power. Yet nothing at all of that is [in reality] the action or the creation of the painter; it is part of the creation of Another. The most that [the artist] can be said to have done is to bring paint and wall together in a particular configuration. Your wonderment and admiration [of God, the Divine Artist,] should be all the greater when you consider that the sperm-drop had been non-existent before its Creator created it in loins and thoraxes; then extracted it and shaped it, making its shape refined; measured it, to the finest measure; formed it in the finest form; divided similar parts of it into different parts; strengthened the bones around its sides; beautified the forms of its members; adorned its outside and inside. He set in order its veins and nerves, making them channels for their nutrition and so making them the means of survival for [the sperm-drop]. He endowed it with powers of hearing, sight, knowledge, and speech. He made for it the spine, to form the foundation of the body; the belly, to contain the alimentary organs; and the head, as the collecting-point (*jāmi'*) for its senses.

43 Qur'ān 79:27-29.

[Furthermore, God] caused the eyes to open up, and arranged the layers [of which they are composed], giving them beauty of form, colour and structure; and He then gave them lids to cover, protect, and clean them and to keep foreign bodies away from them. Moreover, He caused to appear within the [tiny] size of a lens inside them the form of the heavens in the full vastness of their dimensions and the distance between their extremities, so that one can behold them.

Furthermore, He caused the ears to open up, placed in them a bitter liquid to protect their hearing and keep parasites away from them, and surrounded them with auricles in order to collect sounds and direct them back towards the auditory meatus; and also to sense the crawling of any parasite. He also put twists and turns inside it, in order to lengthen the way for [any parasite seeking to enter] it; and to awaken a sleeping person if any creature tried [to enter his ear] while they were asleep.

Next, [God] raised the nose above the centre of the face, giving it a fine form, and opened up two nostrils for it. He imparted to it the olefactory sense in order that one should be able to tell about one's meals and foodstuffs from their smell, and to enable one to breathe fresh air in through them, as food for one's heart and to relieve one's inward heat.

He also opened up the mouth, placing inside it the tongue to speak and to interpret and articulate whatever is in the heart. He adorned the mouth with teeth to act as instruments for grinding, breaking, and cutting; provided them with firm roots and sharp edges; made them white in colour; and arranged them in even rows with edges that are level and symmetrical with each other as if they were a row of finely-strung pearls.

Furthermore, He created the lips, giving them beauty of colour and form, to fit over the mouth and close off that orifice, and also to enable some letters [to be pronounced] in speaking. He created the throat, equipping it to produce sounds; and created in the tongue the power to make movements and disjunctions in order for sounds to emanate from various different points so as to differentiate between letters, enabling a wide range of utterances to be made thanks to their sizeable number. Again, He created larynxes with variations of form in respect to breadth and narrowness, roughness and smoothness, hardness and gentleness, loudness (*ṭūl*) and softness (*qaṣr*), in order that by this means [all] voices would be different. For no two voices are alike; indeed, there is an apparent differentiation between any two voices, so that in the darkness anyone hearing a voice can tell people from one another simply by their voice.

Then [God] adorned the head with hairs and with the temples, and adorned the face with the beard and eyebrows; He adorned the eyebrows with fine hairs and an arched shape; and He adorned the eyes with lashes.

Then [God] created the internal organs, employing each for a specific task. He tasked the stomach with digesting food, the liver with conveying nutrition to the blood, and put the spleen, gall-bladder, and kidney[44] at the service of the liver. The spleen serves it by drawing black bile away from it, the gall-bladder by drawing yellow bile away from it, and the kidney by drawing water away from it; and the bladder serves the kidney by receiving the water from it, and then removes it by way of the urethra. The veins also serve the liver in transporting blood to the other parts of the body.

Then [God] created the hands [and arms], making them long enough to be extendable for [any desired] purposes. He made the palms of the hands broad, and divided the [part extending beyond the palm into] five fingers, divided each [of the four] fingers into three joints, and set the four [fingers] on one side and the thumb on another so that the thumb could reach around all of them. Had the first and the last [generations of mankind] combined [their efforts] in detailed consideration to devise an alternative arrangement for the fingers, other than that whereby the thumb is at a distance from the four [fingers], and the latter are of differing lengths and are aligned in a single row, they could not have succeeded. Thanks to this arrangement, the hand is enabled to grasp and to give. If one extends it, one has a surface upon which to place whatever one wishes; if one compacts it, one has an instrument with which to strike; if one partially bends it, one has a cup; and if one extends it and bends the fingers, one has a scoop.

Then [God] created nails at the tips of the fingers, to beautify

44 It is not clear why the author has 'kidney' in the singular here.

them and as a support behind them to prevent them from being [accidentally] cut and in order to cut up fine things which the fingertips could not deal with, and also for scratching the body when necessary. So were it not for the nails, which are the coarsest parts of the body, if one were to develop an itch he would be the most feeble and helpless of creatures and no other [part] could take its place and scratch his body for him! He then He guided the hand to the place that itches, so that it could reach out to it, even during sleep or unconsciously without any need to be asked. If one had to seek someone else's help, they would not be able to locate the itch except after prolonged exertions.

Once again, [remember that God] created all of this from a sperm-drop, which is [then kept] inside the womb '*in threefold [depths of] darkness*.'[45] If the covering and wrapping could be removed and the eyesight could extend into it, then one could see the designing and formation appearing in it, one thing after another; yet one would not see the Form-Giver or any tools. Have you ever seen anyone who shapes things or does anything without touching his tools or his work or [even] being in contact with them while working on them? Incomparably Glorious is He! How mighty is His Glory, how manifest His Evidence!

Next, consider the perfection of [God's] Omnipotence together with the completeness of His Compassion: how when the womb becomes constrictive for the [unborn] child as it grows, He guides it to a way to turn and move about, and to emerge from that constriction, to seek a way through, as though it possessed the intelligence and the insight to [realise] what it needs.

Next, [consider how] after [the infant] has emerged and is in need of nutrition, [God] guides it to feed at the [mother's] breast; and because its body is feeble and cannot endure dense foodstuffs, how He takes care of it by creating delicate milk. He causes it to emerge, pure and delicate, from '*between filth and blood*';[46] and He created the breasts and concentrated the milk in them, forming in them nipples of a suitable size for the infant's mouth to fit with it.

---

45 Qur'ān 39:6.

46 Qur'ān 16:66.

Again, He opened up in the nipple an extremely narrow opening, in order that the milk not escape except when gradually sucked upon; for an infant can only take in a little [at a time]. Then [consider] how [God] guided it to suck in order to extract abundant milk through that narrow [opening] when very hungry.

Next, consider [God's] tenderness and compassion: how He postponed the creation of the teeth until the completion of the two years [of breastfeeding], since for those two years [the infant] cannot feed on anything but milk and so has no need of teeth. Then, once it has grown [that much] and simple milk is no longer suitable for it, and it needs solid food, and that food requires breaking up and chewing, [God] causes its teeth to grow now that it needs them – neither before then, nor after. Peerless is He in His Perfection, how He produces those solid bones in those soft gums!

Then, [God] aroused tenderness towards [the infant] in his parents to be prepared to take care of him at a time when he is incapable of caring for himself. Were it not that God Most High causes mercy to govern their hearts, the child would be the most incapable of all creatures of looking after himself.

Then consider how [God] provided [the child] with abilities (*qudra*), discernment, intelligence, and guidance – all by degrees – so that he matures and develops, becoming an adolescent, then a youth, then a mature adult, and then an old man. [All this] whether he be thankless or thankful, obedient or disobedient, a believer or an unbeliever, in accordance with the Words of [God] the Exalted: '*Did there pass for man an era of time when he was nothing [to be] remembered? We created man from a sperm-drop of mixed fluid, to put him to the test, and made him able to see and hear. Truly We have guided him towards the Way, whether he be thankful or thankless.*'[47] Look at the kindness and generosity and, furthermore, the omnipotent power and wisdom; you will be dazzled by the marvels of the Divine Presence!

Truly the wonder of all wonders is this: that someone who sees a beautiful inscription or picture on a wall thinks highly of it and then focuses all his concern upon thinking about the artist or calligrapher: how he drew or wrote it, how he was able to achieve it,

---

47 Qur'ān 76:1-3.

continually marvelling inwardly at him and saying, 'What a skilful [artist]! How perfect is his creativity, how excellent his execution!' Yet he is heedless of his own Maker and Shaper, and so fails to be astonished at His Magnificence, or to be staggered by His Glory and Wisdom!

[All] this, then, is [merely] a small part of the wonders of your body. These cannot be dismissed as something remote. They offer the nearest scope available for you to reflect upon and the clearest evidence of the Magnificence of your Creator. Yet you are heedless of that, preoccupied as you are with your belly and your genitals. All you know about yourself is that when you are hungry you eat; when you are sated, you sleep; when you feel lustful, you have intercourse; and when you are angry, you fight. Those are things which all animals know as well as you do! The special privilege of human beings, from which the animal kingdom is barred, is [gaining] knowledge (*maʿrifa*) of God, Exalted is He, by observing *'the Dominion of the heavens and earth'*[48] and the wonders *'on the horizons and within souls'*.[49] That is how a servant [of God] may enter the company of the Angels of Proximity [to God] and be resurrected in the company of the Prophets and those of perfected faith (*ṣiddīqūn*), being brought near to the Presence of the Lord of the Universe. And that is not the [spiritual] station of the animal kingdom, or of a human being who is content with the worldly portion enjoyed by [mere] animals. Truly it is far worse than that of any beast, for they have no ability to [attain] that. For [any human being], on the other hand, God created [that] capacity – which he then failed to put to use, thus rejecting the Divine generosity in [granting] it. *'Those are like cattle – indeed, they are further astray in [their] ways.'*[50]

Now that you are aware of the way to reflect on yourself, contemplate the Earth, which is your dwelling-place; and, moreover, its rivers and seas, mountains and minerals. Then, raise your [thoughts] upwards from them to the domain of the Heavens.

---

48 Qur'ān 6:75 and 7:185.

49 A reference to Qur'ān 41:53.

50 See, with slightly different wording, Qur'ān 7:179 and 25:44.

Signs of God in Creation (apart from human beings)

As for the earth, amongst [God's] signs] is that He created the Earth *'as an expanse'*[51] and *'a flat expanse,*[52] and threaded through it broad pathways, making it easily accessible, so [that you might] *'walk in its tracts.'*[53] He made it stable, so that it does not shift, and anchored it with mountains as pegs for it, lest it should shake.[54] He made its extremities so vast that no human is capable of reaching every part of it, however long their lifetime and however extensive their travels. [As] He has said, Exalted is He, *'And the sky We have raised with Hands [of indescribable immensity], and in truth We are Makers of vastness; and the Earth We have unrolled, and what wondrous Outspreaders [are We]!'*[55] He said also, Exalted is He: *'He it is Who has made the Earth amenable to you, so [you may] walk in its tracts;'*[56] and *'He Who made the Earth an expanse for you.'*[57] Indeed, in His Mighty Book [God] has spoken many times of the Earth, so that its marvels may be reflected upon. Its back is a dwelling-place for the living and its belly a resting-place for the dead. As God says, Exalted is He: *'Have We not made the Earth a habitat, for the dead and for the living?'*[58]

So, then, consider the Earth and [the fact] that it is *dead, but when We send down water upon it, it stirs and swells,*[59] becomes verdant, and grows wonderful plants; and [all] kinds of living creatures come forth from it. Then consider how He strengthened the flanks[60] of the Earth with firm mountains, solid, massive, towering peaks; how He placed bodies of water beneath it, causing springs to gush forth and waters to flow upon it. [He also] brought forth from dry rocks and

51 Qur'ān 2:22.
52 Qur'ān 78:6.
53 Qur'ān 67:15.
54 See Qur'ān 16:15, 21:31, 31:10, 78:7, for references to mountains as pegs to prevent the Earth shaking.
55 Qur'ān 51:48.
56 Qur'ān 67:15.
57 Qur'ān 2:22.
58 Qur'ān 77:25-26.
59 Qur'ān 22:5, 41:39.
60 Or regions (Arabic: *jawānib*).

turbid dust delicate, crystal-clear water by which He made all things that live. He produced all manner of trees and plants: '*grains, vines and fresh vegetation, olive trees and date palms*,'[61] and pomegranates, and countless [types] of fruits of different forms, colours, tastes, smells, and [other] qualities. '*He makes some of them superior to others for eating*,' '[*even if*] *all are watered from one* [*and the same*] *water*'[62] and grow on a single [piece of] land. You may say, '[But] the differences between them arise from the differences between their seeds and roots;' but when was there [ever] in a [date-]stone a palm-tree weighed down with clusters of fresh dates, or when were there [ever] in a single seed '*seven ears, with one hundred grains in each ear*'?[63]

Next, consider the semi-desert lands (*bawādī*), examining their outside and inside. You will see it to be earth that is uniform in appearance. Yet when [God] sends down water upon it, *it quivers and swells, causing every [kind of] delightful pair to grow*[64]; '*varying in colour*',[65] and '*vegetation alike and not alike*',[66] each one differing from the other in taste, scent, colour, and form. Then consider how abundant they are, the differences between their types, their many [diverse] forms; and again, the diverse natures of the plant kingdom, their many uses, and how God Most High has placed [in them] amazing pharmacological properties. This plant gives nutrition, this one gives strength, this one revives, this one kills, this one cools, this one heats, when this one collects in the stomach it draws the yellow bile from the depths of the veins, this one changes into yellow bile, this one attracts phlegm and black bile, this one changes into both of them, this one purifies the blood, this one changes into blood; this one exhilarates, this one is soporific, this one strengthens, and this one weakens. Not one shoot or leaf grows from the earth that does not contain benefits whose essential nature human beings are powerless to grasp!

Now, to raise each one of these plants the farmer needs to

---

61 Qur'ān 80:27-29.

62 Qur'ān 13:4.

63 Qur'ān 2:261.

64 Qur'ān 22:5; also cf. 41:39.

65 Qur'ān 16:13, 16:69, 35:27, 35:28, 39:21.

66 Qur'ān 6:99.

perform a particular task. Date-palms have to be pollinated, vines to be emptied, and crops to be kept free from weeds and undergrowth. Some of that [husbandry] is done by sowing seeds in the soil, some by planting twigs, and some by grafting onto trees. If we wanted to mention [all] the different types, varieties, uses, natural states, and marvels of plants, [entire] days would not suffice to describe [the whole of] that. [But] a brief consideration of each type is sufficient to lead you along the path of reflection. These, then, are the wonders of the vegetable kingdom.

Also among His Signs are the gems buried under the mountains and the minerals extracted from mines. The Earth contains *adjoining regions*[67] [that are] different. Consider the mountains, how exquisite jewels [and metals] are extracted from them: gold, silver, turquoise, rubies, and so on. Some of them are malleable with hammers, like gold, silver, copper, lead, and iron; others are non-malleable, like turquoise and ruby. [Consider also] how God Most High guided mankind to extracting and refining them, and to making vessels, tools, coins, and jewellery from them.

Then consider [other categories of] minerals from the Earth: naphtha, sulphur, tar, and others. The least of them is salt, which is only required to enhance the flavour of food; but if any land were devoid of it, destruction would quickly overtake it.[68] Consider, then, the Mercy of God, Exalted is He: how He created some areas of land as natural saltpans, in such a way that pure rain-water collects in them and so saline, caustic salt is dissolved – of which one could not stomach even a *mithqāl*[69] [by itself] – in order for that to be a condiment for your food when you eat it, adding savour to your life.

[In fact] there is no inanimate being, no animal, and no plant that does not contain some wisdom or power of this kind. None of them were created as a pastime, for amusement, or in jest. Rather, each one was created 'with Truth', as was fitting, in a befitting style, and as befits [God's] Majesty, Generosity, and Subtle Grace; for which reason He says, Exalted is He, *'And We did not create the*

67 See Qur'ān 13:4.

68 Salt is much the most important natural source of sodium, and the minimum daily amount of sodium required to keep a human being alive is 500 mg. In pre-modern times fewer foods contained salt.

69 Equivalent to less than 5 grams.

Heavens and Earth and what lies between them to amuse Ourselves. We created them only in Truth.'[70]

Among His Signs, too, are [all] the species of living creatures, their division into those that fly and those that walk, and the categorisation of those that walk [or crawl] into those which move on two legs, on four, on ten - or [even] on a hundred, as can be found with some small insects; and, furthermore, their division [into sub-categories] according to their use, form, shape, behaviour (*akhlāq*), and nature. Consider the birds in the sky, the wild beasts of the Earth, and the domesticated animals: you will see in them such wonders as leave no room for doubt as to the Magnificence of their Creator, the Omnipotent Power of their Designer (*Muqaddir*), or the Wisdom of their Form-Giver. How could [all] that [ever] be studied exhaustively? Indeed, if we wished to speak of the wonders of the gnat, ant, bee, or spider, which are among the smallest of living creatures – about the building of their homes, how they collect their food, their courtship of their mates, how they store [things] for themselves, their skill in the architecture of their dwellings, and in the manner in which they are guided to [meeting] their own needs, we would not be capable of doing so.

See how the spider builds its home at the side of a road or river. First it looks for two spots close to each other, with a gap of a cubit or less between them, to make it possible for it to bridge the two sides with a thread. It begins by drawing its saliva, of which its thread is composed, around one end in order to fasten it. Next, it passes over to the other end of the thread in order to fasten the other end of it. It then repeats the operation, [making] a second time and a third, thus creating an geometrical connection between [the two ends]. Once it has secured the knots in the rope (*qimṭ*), and arranged the threads into a warp, it gets to work on the weft, adding one part to another and fastening the knot to the point where the weft meets the warp. Throughout the whole of that operation it maintains the geometrical symmetry. Having fashioned it into a web for gnats and flies to fall into, it sits in a corner and waits for some prey to fall into the web. When prey arrives, [the spider] swoops to seize and devour it. If it is unable to catch any quarry in that way, it finds

70 Qur'ān 44:38-39.

itself a corner of a wall and links the two ends of the corner with a thread. It then hangs by another thread and remains suspended in midair while waiting for a fly to come flying by. When that happens, [the spider] throws itself upon it and catches it, wrapping a thread around its legs to hold it fast, before eating it.

There exists no creature, great or small, that does not contain innumerable wonders! Do you suppose that [the spider] learned this skill by itself? Or that it came into existence by itself; or that a human being brought it into existence, or taught it? Or that it had no guide or teacher? Can any perceptive individual doubt that [the spider] is lowly, weak, and powerless? But if the elephant, an enormous creature whose strength is manifest, is incapable of [knowing of its own accord] what to do, how could that feeble creature? Does not that [spider], with its structure, its form, its movements, its direction, and its wondrous handiwork, testify to its own Infinitely Wise Deviser, its All-Powerful and Omniscient Creator? Any perceptive individual will see, therefore, that in this tiny creature there is [sufficient proof of] the Might and the Majesty of its Planner and Creator and the perfection of His Power and Wisdom to leave the mind and understanding awestruck - to say nothing of [the marvels of] all other living creatures.

This subject, too, is [potentially] endless, the [Earth's] creatures being innumerable in their forms, ways and characteristics. [People's] hearts have only lost their sense of wonder at them because of familiarity from having seen them [for themselves]. Indeed, when one sees a strange creature, even if it be a worm, his wonderment is renewed and he will exclaim 'Incomparably Glorious is God! How wondrous is He!' The human being is the most wondrous of living creatures, yet he does not wonder at himself. Yet if he were to consider the grazing animals which he has domesticated, observing their shapes and forms, then their uses and benefits – their hides, wool, fur, and hair, which God created for clothing for His [human] creation and shelters for them whether travelling or at home, as vessels for their drinks and containers for their foods, and as protection for their feet; and how [God] made their milk and meat nutrition for them; and again, how He made some of them beautiful riding mounts and some carriers of loads, traversing distant valleys and wildernesses – the one contemplating [all this] would surely increase in wonder at the Wisdom of their Creator and Form-Giver. For He did not create them except with knowledge that encompassed all of their benefits and preceded His creation of them.

Incomparably Glorious, then, is He in Whose Knowledge all things are disclosed without contemplation (*tafakkur*), reflection (*taʾammul*), or pondering (*tadabbur*), and without seeking the help of a vizier or adviser. For He is the All-Knowing, the All-Aware, the All-Wise, the All-Powerful. By the most minimal part of [all] that He has created, He has drawn from the hearts of those with direct knowledge sincere testimony to His Oneness. Hence mankind cannot do otherwise than to submit to His Overpowering Might and Omnipotent Power, acknowledge His Lordship, and confess their inability to know [completely] His Majesty and Magnificence. Who could [ever] completely enumerate the praise due to Him? Rather, He is as He has praised Himself, and the farthest limit of our knowledge is to confess to [our] inability to know Him. And so We ask God, Exalted is He, to generously bestow on us His guidance, out of His inestimable grace and kindness.

Among His Signs, too, are the deep seas which surround [all] the regions of the Earth, these being parts of the Greater Ocean which surrounds the whole Earth. In fact, all the valleys and hills that are visible above water [level], compared with [all the Earth's] water, are like a small island in a vast sea; and the remainder of the Earth is covered with water. Said the Prophet, may God exalt and preserve him: 'The land in [proportion to] the sea is like a stable in [proportion to] the Earth.'[71] So compare the size of a stable in relation to that of the whole Earth, and realise that the Earth in relation to the seas is equally [tiny]. You have now contemplated [for yourself] the wonders of the land and what it contains. Now reflect on the wonders of the sea. For the wonders of the sea, and the gems and living creatures in it, exceed [many] times over those you can see on the face of the Earth, just as its extent exceeds that of the [dry] land.

Truly the mightiest aspect of the Ocean is the huge creatures

---

71 According to *Itḥāf al-sāda*, the Traditionist al-ʿIrāqī found no source for this in any Hadith compilation.

whose backs can be seen in the sea. One might think it was an island, so that travellers could land on it – but then it may sense fires when they burst into flame, and begin to move so that it becomes evident that it is a creature. Furthermore, there is no category of land animal, be it a horse, bird, cow, or human being, that does not have multiple equivalents in the sea - as well as species not resembling anything to be found on land. These have been described in volumes and collected by peoples who are concerned with travelling the sea and collecting its marvels.

Next, consider how God, Incomparably Glorious and Exalted is He, created pearls, turning them round in their shells beneath the water. Consider, too, how He caused coral to grow from solid rocks under water; and it is actually a plant with the structure of a tree, growing out of rock.[72] Then, consider other [phenomena]: ambergris and the various types of precious substance which the sea casts up and are extracted from it.

Next, consider the wonders of ships [and boats], how God Most High keeps them on the surface of the water and has allowed traders, those in quest of riches, and others to travel in them. He has subjected to them vessels that carry their cargoes, then dispatched the winds to drive ships along, and has additionally acquainted sailors with [the winds'] origins, directions, and seasons.

All the wonders of God's creation in the seas could never be described in their entirety, [even] in [multiple] volumes. Yet more amazing than all of that is something that is more readily visible than anything [else] there is to be seen: the nature of a drop of water. It is a delicate, subtle, fluid, transparent body comprising parts that are joined as though they were a single thing, subtle (*laṭīf*) in its composition, amenable to control (*taṣarruf*), and susceptible both of dispersion and of connection. [Water] is the means of life for every creature and every plant on the face of the Earth. So if a [human] servant [of God] was in need of a drink of a water but was unable to get one, he would give away all the treasuries of the Earth and the kingship of the world to obtain it, if it was in his power to. Again, if after drinking it he was [later] unable to excrete it, he would give away all the treasuries of the Earth and the kingship of

72 Most corals consist of vast numbers of tiny creatures, called polyps.

the world [for the ability] to excrete!

How strange it is, therefore, how highly human beings esteem the [gold] dinar, the [silver] dirham, and fine jewels and yet they are heedless of the bounty of God Most High in a drink of water whenever they need to drink or excrete it – even though they would give the whole world away for it!

So, then, ponder the wonders of waters and rivers, wells and oceans; for they contain extensive scope for reflection. All of those things are mutually supporting pieces of evidence and mutually reinforcing signs that speak with the tongue of their state, eloquently extolling the Majesty of their Maker, expressing the Perfect Wisdom that they contain, calling out to those with [open] hearts with their melodious songs, addressing every thinking person: 'Can you not see me - see my form, my composition and attributes, my uses, my various states, and the number of my benefits? Do you suppose that I came into being of my own accord, or that one of my kind created me? Are you not ashamed that you look at a word written with three letters, and then assert that they are the work of a human being who has knowledge, ability, will and speech – then you look at the marvels of the Divine calligraphy written on the pages of my face with the Divine Pen, of which eyesight cannot perceive the nature, movement or point of contact with the [written] line; and yet your heart is far removed from [grasping] the Majesty of its Maker?'

Again, the sperm-drop says to those who possess hearts and hearing, not to '*those dismissed from hearing*',[73] 'Imagine me in the darkness of the innards, immersed in menstrual blood, at the time when the design and formation appear on my face. The [Divine] artist delineates my pupils, eyelids, forehead, cheeks, and lips, and you see the drawn forms (*nuqūsh*) gradually appear, one after another.' And yet you cannot see any artist [at work] either inside or outside the sperm-drop[74], or inside or outside the womb; nor have the mother or father, the embryo, or the womb, the least awareness of [all this]. Is not this artist, then, more wondrous than one whom you can

73 See Qur'ān 26:212, where this expression is used in a different context about some of the jinn.

74 For Ghazālī to speak of 'the sperm-drop' here, rather than the embryo, is surprising; it may possibly be for rhetorical purposes, underlining the minuteness of the organism on which the Divine Artist operates.

watch as he draws a wonderful picture with [his] pen? If you look at it once or twice you will know [what] it [looks like]; but are you capable of knowing that kind of [real-life] drawing and painting, which involves both the outside and the inside of the embryo and all of its parts without touching the embryo or having any contact with it either from within or from outside?

But [what] if you are not amazed at these wonders and cannot understand from them that the One Who formed, delineated and made [them] to precise measurements (*qaddara*) has no peer, and that no delineator or painter is His equal, Infinitely Perfect is He, just as His designing and craftsmanship is unequalled by [any other] designing and craftsmanship, the distinction and vast disparity between the [respective] actors being equal to that between their actions? If you do not wonder at [all] this, then be amazed at your own lack of wonderment, for it is more amazing than any wonder! He Who has blinded your insight in the face of this clear, straightforward [evidence] and prevent you from having certainty in the face of this descriptive explanation is indeed most deserving to be wondered at!

Incomparably Glorious, then, is He Who guides and misguides, leads astray and leads aright, destines [eternal] damnation or felicity; Who opens up the insight of those He loves so that they behold Him in every single part and particle of the Universe; and Who renders the hearts of His enemies blind, veiling Himself from them in His Glory and Exaltedness! '*His are the Creation and the Command*,'[75] [all] Favour (*minna*) and Grace (*faḍl*), Kindness (*luṭf*) and All-Prevailing Might (*qahr*). None can rescind His Decree, and none can countermand His Decision.

Also among His Signs is the subtle air that is trapped in between the concavity of the sky and the convexity of the Earth; its substance (*jism*) can be perceived by the sense of touch when the wind blows, but its form (*shakhṣ*) cannot be seen by the eyes. In its totality it is like a single ocean in which the birds, circling and racing '*in the air of the sky*,'[76] 'swim' with their wings as aquatic creatures swim in the water; and when the wind blows, pockets (*jawānib*) and waves [of air] are stirred up like the waves of the sea. And when God moves

75 Qur'ān 7:54.

76 Qur'ān 16:79.

the air, causing a wind to blow, if He so wills He makes it '*good news in advance of His Mercy*'[77] - as He says, Incomparably Glorious is He: '*And We send the winds as pollinators*'[78]– so that through its movement the refreshing influence (*rawḥ*) of air reaches animals and plants and so they are made ready for growth. Or else, if He so wishes, He makes [winds] a [means of] punishment for those of His creation who are disobedient. As He says, Exalted is He: '*We unleashed against them a howling wind, on a day of endless horror, which swept people away like uprooted trunks of palm-trees*.'[79]

Next, consider the subtleness of the air, and also its force and strength when compressed in water: [even] a strong man struggling with an inflated waterskin to [try to] submerge it in the water will not be able to; but when solid iron is placed on the surface of water it will sink in it. Consider, then, how air is kept out of (*yunqabiḍ min*) water by virtue of its strength combined with its subtleness; by this wisdom [or 'natural law'], [God] Most High holds ships up on the surface of the water. In the same way, anything hollow that contains air will not sink in the water because the air is kept from sinking in water and does not separate from the inner surface of the ship. Thus a heavy ship, despite its power and solidity, remains suspended from the subtle air, like someone who, when on the point of falling into a well, clings to the coat-tails of a strong man who is preventing [him] from falling down the well. Thus the ship, with its concavity, clings on by the 'coat-tails' of the strong air to prevent it from sinking and falling down in the water.[80] Glorious in His Utter Perfection is He Who keeps a heavy ship suspended in the subtle air, without any visible connection or fastened knot!

77 Qur'ān 25:48, 27:63.

78 Qur'ān 15:22.

79 Qur'ān 54:19-20.

80 Considering the extent of Ghazālī's scientific knowledge, by the standards of his time, it is rather surprising that he seems not to have been aware of, or at any rate understood, the law of hydrostatics (buoyancy) first articulated, as far as we can know, by Archimedes about thirteen centuries earlier.

[What is between the Heavens and the Earth]

Next, consider the wonders of the air and of [the phenomena] manifested there: clouds and mist, thunder, lightning, rain, snow, meteors, and thunderbolts (*ṣawāʿiq*). These are the wonders of what is between Heaven and Earth. The Qurʾān has alluded to all of them, where [God] says, Exalted is He: '*We did not create the Heavens, the Earth, and what is between them, for [mere] recreation.*'[81] Those [things just referred to] are 'what is between them'. The Qurʾān refers to individual aspects of them in various passages, [for example] when [God] says, Glorious Speaker that He is: '[*In the turning about of the winds*] *and the clouds,* [*Divinely*] *controlled between the Heavens and the Earth,* [*are signs for thinking people*],'[82] and where He speaks of thunder and lightning, and clouds and rain. But if you gain from the whole of this nothing more than seeing the rain with your eyes and hearing the thunder with your ears, that is [a mode of] knowledge which the animal kingdom shares with you. Therefore you should raise yourself up from this lowly world of the animals to the Realm of the Supreme Assembly [in Heaven].[83] You have opened your eyes and so have perceived the things mentioned above in their outward appearance; [now] close your outward eyes and look with your interior vision. Then you will behold their inward wonders and their extraordinary secrets.

This too is a subject area on which one may reflect at length. However, since it is not desirable to explore it fully [here], simply consider the thick, dark clouds: how you see them gather in the clear, pure air; how God Most High creates them as and when He will; how [the clouds], fragile as they are, carry water which is heavy, moving about in the sky until God allows them to fall to the Earth, dividing them up into raindrops, each one in the size and form He wishes. You will see a cloud scattering water on the Earth, dropping it as individual drops, none of which either touches or combines with any other. Instead, every single [drop] descends by

81 Qurʾān 21:16, 44:38.

82 Qurʾān 2:164.

83 The Supreme Assembly (*al-Malaʾ al-Aʿlā*) comprises the Archangels and other beings in close proximity to the Divine Presence: see Qurʾān 38:69, etc.

the route designated for it, from which it never deviates; the one behind never moves ahead, nor does the one in front move back, until they fall on the ground, drop by drop. If the ancients and the moderns were to join forces to create a single drop, or to determine the number of drops that fall in a single region (*balda*) or in a single village, jinns and humans alike would be powerless to count them; only He Who brought them into existence knows their number. Moreover, every drop has been assigned to a spot on Earth and to the creatures there: birds, wild animals, and all [kinds of] insects and beasts (*dawābb*). Upon that raindrop it is written, in Divine writing invisible to outward vision, that it [for instance] is the provision for such-and-such a worm which is in the direction (*nāḥiya*) of a certain hill, and will reach it when it is thirsty, at a certain time. There are innumerable [other] wonders, [such as] the freezing of water into hard, solid ice and the dispersion of snowflakes like carded cotton.

All this is a bounty from the All-Powerful Dominator, part of the irresistible Might of God, the Ever-Creating Subjugator, in which none of His creatures has any part or influence. Hence, in those who are believers, His creation can only give rise to humility and submission to His Majesty and Greatness; in the blindly contentious, on the other hand, it gives rise only to ignorance as to its nature (*kayfiyya*) and mere guesswork as regards the cause and origin [of natural phenomena]. So it is that an ignorant person may say, in error: 'Water falls only because it is heavy by nature, and that is the only reason why it falls' - thinking that this is a piece of knowledge which he has discovered, and congratulating himself on it. But if he were asked what 'nature' means; what created it; what created the water that is heavy by nature; what it was that raised water which had fallen, as rain, to the lowest parts of a tree up to its highest branches despite [the water] being heavy by nature; how it descends to the bottom and is then raised to the top inside the trees, a little at a time and in a manner that cannot be seen or observed, until it is distributed to every part of its leaves, nourishing every part of each one, which it reaches by running through tiny, hair-thin veins.[84] One can see the vein which is the 'trunk' (*aṣl*) of the leaf; then from that

---

84 Only at this point does Ghazālī's indirect question end, to be replaced by plain factual statement.

large vein which extends along its [entire] length, run smaller veins. It is as if the large [vein] were a river, and those which branch off from it were rivulets, then the rivulets branched off into tiny stems (*sawāq*) that are smaller than it, then they branched off into thin, gossamer-like (*'ankabūtiyya*) threads invisible to the eye. Thus [the pathways] extend across the entire breadth of the leaf, and through its interior water reaches all parts of the leaf, nourishing it, fostering its growth, and beautifying it. Its moist freshness and bloom persist. The same applies to all the parts of fruit.

But if the natural movement of water is downwards, how is it able to move upwards? And if that is due to some attractive force, what activates that attractive force? If all of this, in the final analysis, is due to the Creator of the Heavens and Earth, the All-Compelling [Master] of the Sensory Domain (*Mulk*) and the Spiritual Domain (*Malakūt*), why not credit it to Him in the first place? The finishing-point of the ignorant is the starting-point of the intelligent!

The Heavens

Amongst His Signs are the realm of the heavens and the stars which they contain, which is the whole of the matter (*al-amr kulluh*)! Anyone who perceives the totality without considering the wonders of the heavens has verifiably (*taḥqīqan*) failed to consider the totality. In fact, in proportion to the heavens, the Earth, the seas, the air, and every single body apart from the heavens are like a drop in the ocean, or less. Furthermore, consider the value which God gives in His Book to the stars and other heavenly bodies; there is not one Sūra that does not praise them in various passages.[85] How many times they are sworn by in the Qur'ān! He says, for example, Exalted is He: '*By the sky with its constellations*',[86] '*By the sky and the Night Visitor*',[87] '*By the sky with its pathways*',[88] '*By the sky and Him Who*

85 This is not literally the case, although many Sūras do.

86 Qur'ān 85:1.

87 Qur'ān 86:1.

88 Qur'ān 51:7.

built it',[89] '*By the sun and its morning brightness; and by the moon when it follows it*',[90] '*I swear by the receding [planets]*,'[91] '*By the star when it sets*,'[92] and '*No: I swear by the setting-places of the stars; and that is indeed a mighty oath, did you but know*.'[93]

You already know that the ancients and the moderns are incapable of knowing the wonders of a base sperm-drop, but God has not sworn by that [in the Qur'ān]! What do you think, then, about by which God Most High has sworn, and to which He assigns and attributes the things with which you have been provided in advance, saying: '*And in Heaven is your provision and that which you are promised*'[94]? He praises those who reflect upon it, saying: '*...and who reflect upon the creation of the Heavens and Earth*.'[95] Said the Emissary of God: 'Woe to him who recites this verse, then wipes his moustache with it'[96] – that is, who continues [reciting] without reflecting on it. Also, [God] criticizes those who turn away from [such Signs] in these Words: '*And the sky We raised as a roof well protected, yet they keep turning away from His Signs!*'[97] What have the Heavens in common with all the land and sea on Earth? The latter are constantly (*'alā al-qurb*) changing; the Heavens, however, are solid, strong, and protected from changing until 'The Book [of Divine Decrees] has reached its [destined] term.'[98] That is why God Most High calls it '*well protected*' in His Words '*And the sky We raised as a roof well protected*.'[99] He also says, Transcendently Perfect is He, '*And We built above you seven strong [Heavens]*;'[100] and '*Are you a mightier creation or the sky He built? He raised its canopy and set it in order*.'[101]

---

89 Qur'ān 91:5.

90 Qur'ān 91:1-2.

91 Qur'ān 81:15-16.

92 Qur'ān 53:1.

93 Qur'ān 56:75-76.

94 Qur'ān 51:22.

95 Qur'ān 3:191.

96 This Hadith is found in the *Ṣaḥīḥ* of Ibn Ḥibbān (no. 620) and quoted in *Qūt al-qulūb*, vol. 1, p. 254.

97 Qur'ān 21:32.

98 Cf. Qur'ān 2:235, where the same phrase is used in a very different context.

99 Qur'ān 21:32.

100 Qur'ān 78:12.

101 Or, '*Were you harder to create, or the sky He built*?' See Qur'ān 79:27-28.

Look into the Realms [of God's creation], and you will discover the wonders of [His] Majesty and Omnipotence. Do not think that observing [those] Realms means that you should simply look at them for a long time, noting the azure of the sky, the light and the scatteredness of the stars; the animal kingdom share equally with you in looking at them. If the scope [of observation] were limited to that, why ever would God Most High have praised Abraham by saying '*And thus did We show Abraham the Supernal Domain of the Heavens and Earth*'[102]? Far from it: the Qur'ān refers to all that can be seen by the eyes as 'the Sensory Domain (*Mulk*)' or as 'the Manifest (*al-Shahāda*)'.[103] As for that which is hidden from eyesight, He employs the terms 'the Unseen (*al-Ghayb*)' and 'the Spiritual Domain (*Malakūt*)'. God Most High is '*The Knower of the Unseen and the Manifest*'[104] and the All-Compelling [Lord] of the Kingdom and the Suprasensory Realm; '*they encompass nothing of His Knowledge except as He wills.*'[105] He is '*the Knower of the Unseen, and His Unseen is manifested to no one but a Prophet with whom He is well pleased.*'[106]

O man of intellect, extend your contemplation of the Supernal Domain, so that perhaps the gates of Heaven may be opened to you and you may be able to roam its regions with your heart, until your heart finds itself before the Throne of the All-Merciful. Then you may be able to hope to attain the rank of 'Umar ibn al-Khaṭṭāb,[107] may God be well pleased with him, who said: 'My heart has beheld my Lord.' This is because the attainment of that which is further away can only happen after one has surpassed that which is nearer. The thing that is closest to you is your own self, then the Earth which is your abode, then the air which surrounds you; then the plants, the animals, and everything else that is on the face of the Earth; then the marvels of the air, or of that which is between Heaven and

102 Qur'ān 6:75.

103 These are more commonly referred to as 'the Realm of the Kingdom (*'ālam al-Mulk*)' and 'the Realm of the Manifest (*'ālam al-Shahāda*).

104 See Qur'ān 6:73, 9:105, 13:9, 23:92, 32:6, 39:46, 59:22, 62:8, 64:18.

105 Qur'ān 2:255.

106 Qur'ān 72:26-27.

107 'Umar ibn al-Khaṭṭāb (d. 23/644) was the second caliph and is revered as one of the most saintly and learned of the Prophet's Companions.

Earth; then the seven Heavens and their stars; then the Footstool, the Throne, the Angels who bear the Throne, and the [Angelic] Wardens of the Heavens. From there you will pass on to behold the Lord of the Throne, the Footstool, the Heavens and the Earth, and all that is between them.

Now, between you and these [last-mentioned] things are vast expanses, enormous distances, obstacles that are hard to overcome; and you have yet to overcome the obstacle that is nearest to you, and lowest: that of knowing the outward aspect of yourself. And yet in your insolence you start wagging your tongue and claim to have direct knowledge (*maʿrifa*) of your Lord. 'I have [now] come to know Him and His creation. What [else] should I contemplate and what [else] should I look at?' Lift your head towards the sky right now, and consider it together with its stars, with their orbits and their rising and setting, as well as the sun and the moon it contains, with their various points of rising and setting. Consider how [the heavenly bodies] are continually in motion, without any slowing of their movement or change in their courses; thus it is that they all run together through positions determined by precise determination, never susceptible of increase or decrease until God, Exalted is He, shall '*roll them up like a written scroll.*'[108] Consider the number of the stars, their multitude, their differences of colour – one inclining towards red, one towards white, and one towards the hue of lead. Look at the figures [by which the constellations are recognized and referred to]: Scorpio, Aries, Taurus, Leo, and the Human (*al-Insān*);[109] there is no figure on Earth that does not have a likeness in the Heavens.

Then observe the trajectory of the Sun in its [orbital] sphere for the duration of a year: besides that, each day it rises and ascends, in a second trajectory to which its Creator has subjected it. Were it not for its rising and setting there would be no alternation of night and day, one could not distinguish any seasons, and one would undoubtedly have either perpetual darkness or light; nor could one distinguish between the time

108 Qur'ān 21:104.

109 No constellation with the generic, non-indicative name *al-Insān* has been identified; the others are those of zodiac signs. In the *Kīmiyā* (vol. 2, p. 524) Ghazālī has 'Aries, Taurus, Scorpio, etc.'

for [making] one's living (*ma'āsh*) and the time for resting. Consider how God Most High has made night as a garment, sleep for repose, and daytime for [seeking] provision.'[110] Consider how He '*brings night into day, and day into night*,'[111] thus providing for increase and decrease in each of them in accordance with a specific decree. Consider how He makes the course of the Sun decline (*imāla*) from the middle sky, and how that leads to the variation of the seasons: summer and winter, spring and autumn. When the course of the sun declines below the middle [level] of the sky, the air grows cold and winter appears; when it is in the middle of the sky, the heat is strong; and when it is in between, the weather (*zamān*) is moderate.[112]

We have no desire to enumerate even one-hundredth of a single part of the wonders of the Heavens. What we have described is no more than a suggestion regarding the way of contemplating. Be firm, then, in your conviction that there exists no heavenly body[113] which does not contain many [signs] of the Wisdom of God Most High, in respect of its creation, size, form, colour, position in the sky, closeness to or distance from the middle of the sky, and closeness to or distance from the heavenly bodies adjacent to it. Compare that with what we have said about the members of your body, and that there are none that do not contain some [sign of] wisdom - indeed, many of them. The order of the sky is [something altogether] more immense; in fact there is no common measure (*nisba*) between the terrestrial and the celestial worlds, whether in respect of their size or of the number of their significances (*ma'ānī*). Measure the difference between the two, in respect of the number of their points of significance, based on the disparity in size between the latter and the former. As you are aware, the size of the Earth and the distance between its extremities is too great for any human to be able to perceive it or to follow its circumference.

Observers (*nāẓirūn*) are in agreement that the Sun is more

---

110 Cf. Qur'ān 78:9-11, where the three phrases occur in a different order..

111 Cf. Qur'ān 3:27, 22:61, 31:29, 35:13, 57:6.

112 Or, at least, relatively so in either case, depending of course upon factors such as geographical latitude.

113 The word Ghazālī uses means 'stars', but there can be little doubt that he is referring equally to moons or any kind of celestial body.

than one hundred and sixty times as large as the Earth[114]. There are Traditions that provide indications as to its vastness,[115] and even the smallest stars that one can see are eight times the size of the Earth, while the largest is almost 120 times greater. From this you can grasp their height and distance, even though owing to their remoteness they appear small to your eyes. Indeed, God Most High has alluded to their remoteness in saying, '*He has raised* [*the heavens'*] *canopy and set it in order*.'[116] And it is stated in Traditions that [the distance] between each heaven and the next is [a journey of] five hundred years.[117]

If that is the size of a single star compared with that of the Earth, consider their vast number; then consider the sky in which they are positioned, and its vastness; then consider the rapidity of its movement. You cannot perceive its movement at all, much less its rapidity. Be in no doubt, however, that in an instant it travels a distance equal to the breadth of a star. For the [interval of] time from the rising of the first part of a star to that of the whole of it is brief. Now, in that instant the [heavenly] sphere [containing that star] will have made a turn one hundred times greater than [that of] the Earth.[118] And it revolves in that way continually, while you are unaware of it! Consider how Gabriel, peace be upon him, indicated the speed of his movement when the Prophet, may God exalt and preserve him, asked him, 'Has the sun passed its zenith?' and he replied 'No. Yes!' The Prophet asked him, 'How can you say 'No. Yes!'? [Gabriel] replied, 'Between the moment when I said 'No' and the moment when I said 'Yes!' the Sun made a journey of five hundred years.'[119] So consider the vastness of its form, then the

---

114 The radius of the sun is on average approximately 109 times that of Earth; its volume is 1,304,000 times that of Earth.

115 Including this Hadith in the *Musnad* of Imam Aḥmad ibn Ḥanbal (vol. 2, p. 207), narrated by 'Abd Allāh ibn 'Amr: 'The Emissary of God (may God exalt and preserve him) saw the sun as it set, and he said: 'In the raging Fire of God, but for that which restrains it by God's Command, it would have caused everything on Earth to perish.'

116 Qur'ān 79:28.

117 *Sunan* of al-Tirmidhī, Hadith 2540.

118 Because the sphere, corresponding to the size of that star, will by this reckoning be over a hundred times greater than the relatively slowly rotating Earth.

119 According to *Itḥāf al-sāda*, the Hadith master al-'Irāqī found no source for this purported Hadith, which Ghazālī may have borrowed from Abū Ṭālib al-Makkī's

agility with which it moves. Next, consider the Omnipotence of its All-Wise Creator: how He has accommodated its form, despite the huge distance between its extremities, to fit into the pupil of the eye despite the latter's tiny size, so that while sitting on the ground with your eyes open [and looking] towards it you can see the whole of it.

Such is the sky in its vastness and its multitude of stars. [Now,] however, do not consider that. Instead, consider how its Creator made it and raised it '*Without pillars you* [*can*] *see*'[120] and without there being anything above it for it to hang from. The whole world is like a single house, the sky being its roof. What is astounding about *you* is that when you enter a rich man's house and see it adorned with paint and embellished with gilding, for the rest of your life you never cease to be amazed at it, or to speak about it and describe its beauty – while on the other hand, even though you are always looking at this gigantic house [which is the world], at its floor, its ceiling, its air, the marvellous objects it contains, its extraordinary living creatures and their wonderful design, you never speak of them or even pay any attention to them with your heart! This house is certainly not inferior to that other house that you keep on describing, which is in fact a part of the floor which itself represents the lowest part of this house [of the world]. And yet you do not even look at it! The reason can only be that this is the house of your Lord, which He alone constructed and organised; and you have forgotten yourself, your Lord, and the house of your Lord, being concerned [only] with your belly and your sexual organs; your sole concern being for your own greed and prestige (*ḥashma*). The fullest [possible] extent of your appetite is to fill your belly, but being unable to eat [even] one-tenth of what an animal can consume, the latter is ten times your superior. The fullest [possible] scope of your ability to earn prestige is for ten or a hundred of your acquaintances to come to you and hypocritically flatter you to your face with their tongues while inwardly concealing views concerning you which are disgusting. Even if they are sincere in their affection for you, '*They have no power to bring you or themselves any benefit or harm,*

Qūt al-qulūb (vol. 1, p. 25).

120 Qur'ān 13:2, 31:10.

death or life, or resurrection.'[121]

In your country there may be wealthy Jews and Christians who are higher in [social] rank than you. You may have preoccupied yourself with those vain things and neglected to contemplate the beauty of the Realms of the Heavens and the Earth; you have also neglected to take delight in contemplating the Majesty of the Master of [the Realms of] the Supernal Domain and the Kingdom. You and your intelligence resemble nothing more than an ant which issues forth from the nest it has excavated inside a fortified palace, loftily built, with sturdy pillars, adorned by [the presence of] serving-girls and pageboys and [all] kinds of precious, exquisite objects. When it left its nest and met its friend, it would not speak – if it could speak at all – of anything but its home and its food and how it stores it. As for the palace and the king inside it, it would be far removed from them or thinking about them. In fact, it would be powerless to progress beyond considering itself, its food, and its home to anything else.

Now, just as the ant is heedless of the palace, its floor, ceiling, walls, or the rest of its structure, and is equally uninterested in its residents, so you too are heedless of the house of God Most High and of His Angels who are the inhabitants of His Heavens. You have no knowledge of the Heavens beyond what that ant knows of the roof of its own dwelling, no knowledge of the Angels beyond what that ant knows of you and the [other] inhabitants of your house. But an ant has no means of knowing you, the marvels of your palace, or the wonders of craftmanship which the [Divine] Artist has wrought there. You, on the other hand, possess the [potential] power to roam around the Supernal Domain and become acquainted with such of its wonders as [the generality of] creatures are unaware of.

Let us now pull back on the reins of speaking in this fashion, for there is no end to its scope. Even if we were to spend lengthy lifetimes enlarging on it, we would not be able to explain [in full] what favours God has conferred on us with through knowledge of Him. All that we have come to know is meagre, trifling and paltry compared with what the learned and the saints collectively have come to know; what they have come to know is meagre, trifling and paltry compared with what the Prophets, peace be upon them, have

121 Cf. Qur'ān 25:3.

come to know; all that they have come to know is little compared with what our Prophet Muḥammad, may God exalt and preserve him, came to know; everything that all of the Prophets have come to know is little compared to that which the Angels close [to God], like Isrāfīl, Gabriel, and the others, have come to know. Furthermore, all the types of knowledge possessed by [all] angels, jinn, and mankind, when compared with the Knowledge possessed by God, Incomparably Perfect and Exalted is He, do not deserve [even] to be called 'knowledge': it would be nearer [the mark] for them to be called 'perplexity', 'uncertainty', 'deficiency', and 'incapacity'. All glory, therefore, be to Him Who has made known to His servants whatever He has made known – and has then addressed them, one and all, saying: '*And of knowledge you have been given but little.*'[122]

122 Qur'ān 17:85. The rhetorical use of *tankīr* (indefinite) in *qalīlan* 'a little' implies the meaning 'exceedingly little'.

Conclusion

THAT is an exposition of the general points which the thoughts of those reflecting upon the creation of God Most High should explore. They do not include reflection upon the Entity of God, Exalted is He. Reflecting upon [His] creation, however, leads inevitably to knowledge of the Creator, of His Immensity, Majesty and Omnipotence. The more you know about the wondrous works of God Most High, the more complete will be your knowledge of His Majesty and Immensity. It will be as if, having praised a learned man as a result of finding out about his erudition, you proceeded to discover extraordinary things in his writings or his poems; so that as your knowledge of him increases, so do your reverence, esteem and respect for his [true] worth. His every saying, or every marvellous verse of his poetry, so raises the appreciation for him in your heart that you are compelled to exalt him on your own account. In the same way, you should consider the creating of God Most High; how it has been formed and put together; and how every type of thing that exists was created and formed by Him. The study and contemplation of all that [potentially] accompany each other beyond any limit, though each individual can [only] succeed to the extent allotted to them [by God].

Let us therefore confine ourselves to what we have [already] said, adding what was expounded in detail in the Book of Gratitude.[1] In

1 The Book of Patience and Gratitude (*Kitāb al-Ṣabr wa al-Shukr*) is the second book in the fourth Quarter of the *Iḥyā'*. There is an annotated English translation by H.T. Littlejohn: *Al-Ghazālī on Patience and Thankfulness:* Kitāb al-ṣabr wa 'l-shukr, *Book XXXII of The Revival of the Religious Sciences* (Cambridge, 2010).

that Book we considered the Action of God Most High inasmuch as it is a benefaction and a favour bestowed on us,[2] whereas in this Book we have considered it only inasmuch as it is the Action of God Most High.

Everything that we have considered in [this Book] is [also] considered by the naturalist. But his [manner of] studying it brings about misguidance and [eternal] misfortune, whereas for someone who has received the Divine favour of [spiritual] success, reflecting upon all those things becomes the means of having a correct intention and [eternal] good fortune. Not one particle exists in either the heavens or the Earth whereby God, Transcendently Perfect and Majestic is He, does not misguide whomever He wills and guide whomever He wills.

So it is that anyone who studies those things while considering them as being the Actions and Works of God Most High will thereby gain knowledge of His Glory and His Greatness, and hence they will be rightly guided. On the other hand, anyone who studies them while confining himself to considering them from the viewpoint of how they affect each another, without observing that they are linked to the Cause of all Causes, will be ruined and will have an unhappy destiny. We seek refuge in God from going astray, and we ask Him that we avoid that terrain so treacherous for the feet of the ignorant, by His Grace, Generosity, Favour, Bounty and Compassion.

Here ends the Book of Contemplation, which is the ninth Book of the Quarter of Saving Matters of the Book *The Revival of the Sciences of Religion*. Praise be to God first and last; and exaltation and salutation be upon His Prophet and Family, inwardly and outwardly.

2 That is, on humankind.

Bibliography

Abū Nuʿaym al-Iṣfahānī, Aḥmad ibn ʿAbd Allāh. *Ḥilyat al-awliyāʾ wa Ṭabaqāt al-aṣfiyāʾ*. Beirut, 1987.

Abū al-Shaykh, ʿAbd Allāh ibn Muḥammad. *al-ʿAẓama*. Ed. Riḍā Allāh ibn Muḥammad Idrīs Mubārakfūrī. 2nd ed. Riyadh, 1998.

Aḥmad ibn Ḥanbal. *Musnad al-Imām Aḥmad bin Ḥanbal*. Ed. Shuʿayb al-Arnāʾūṭ. Beirut, 1995.

Aḥmad-i Jām, *Ḥadīqat al-ḥaqīqa*. Ed. Muḥammad ʿAlī Muwaḥḥid. Tehran, 1343 sh./1964.

Al-Attas, Syed Muhammad Naguib. *Prolegomena to the Metaphysics of Islam: an exposition of the fundamental elements of the worldview of Islam*. Kuala Lumpur, 1995.

Anṣārī, ʿAbd Allāh. *Stations of the Sufi Path: the One Hundred Fields (Ṣad maydān) of Abdullah Ansari of Herat*. Tr. Nahid Angha. Bartlow, UK, 2010.

ʿAṭṭār, Farīd al-Dīn Muḥammad ibn Ibrāhīm. *Muṣībat-nāma*. Ed. Muḥammad Riḍā Shafīʿī Kadkanī. Tehran, 1386 sh./2007.

Badri, Malik. *Contemplation: an Islamic Psychospiritual Study*. London, 2000.

Bahāʾ al-Dīn Walad, Muḥammad. *Maʿārif*. Ed. Badīʿ al-Zamān Furūzānfar. 2 vols. Tehran, 1333 sh./1954.

al-Balkhī, Abū Zayd. *Maṣāliḥ al-abdān wa al-anfus*. Ed. Maḥmūd Miṣrī. Cairo, 2005.

———. *Abū Zayd al-Balkhī's Sustenance of the Soul*. Tr. Malik Badri. London and Herndon, VA, 2013.

al-Bayhaqī, Aḥmad ibn al-Ḥusayn. *Kitāb al-Asmāʾ wa l-ṣifāt*. Cairo, 2019.

———. *Shuʿab al-īmān*. Ed. Muḥammad al-Saʿīd ibn Basyūnī Zaghlūl. Beirut, 1410/1990.

Beck, Aaron. *Cognitive Therapy and the Emotional Disorders*. New York, 1976.

Bukhārī, Muḥammad ibn Ismāʿīl. *al-Jāmiʿal-Ṣaḥīḥ*. Beirut, 1422/2001.

Chittick, William C. *The Sufi Path of Knowledge: Ibn al-ʿArabi's Metaphysics of Imagination*. Albany, NY, 1989.

The Colossal Elephant and his Spiritual Feats: Shaykh Ahmad-e Jām, the life and legend of a popular Sufi saint. Tr. and annotated Heshmat Moayyad and Franklin Lewis. Costa Mesa, CA, 2004.

Craig, William Lane. *The* Kalām *Cosmological Argument*. London, 1979.

al-Daylamī, Abū Manṣūr. *al-Firdaws bi-ma'thūr al-khiṭāb* [= *Musnad al-Firdaws*]. Ed. al-Saʿīd ibn Basyūnī Zaghlūl. Beirut, 1986.

De Bruijn, J.T.P. *Of piety and poetry: the interaction of religion and literature in the works of Ḥakīm Sanā'ī of Ghazna*. Leiden, 1983.

———. *Persian Sufi poetry: an introduction to the mystical use of Classical Persian poems*. Richmond, UK, 1997.

al-Ghazālī, Abū Ḥāmid Muḥammad ibn Muḥammad. *al-Ḥikma fī makhlūqāt Allāh ʿazz wa jall*. In: *Majmūʿat rasā'il al-Imām al-Ghazālī*. 6th ed. (Beirut, 1434/2013), pp. 3-54; (Cairo, n.d.), pp. 5-49.

———. *Iḥyā' ʿulūm al-Dīn*. 10 vols. Jeddah, 2011.

———. [Book 1] Kitāb al-ʿilm, *the Book of Knowledge: Book 1 of the* Iḥyā' ʿulūm al-dīn. Tr. Kenneth Honerkamp. Louisville, KY, 2015.

———. [Book 9] *Invocations & Supplications*: Kitāb al-adhkār wa'l-daʿawāt, *Book IX of The Revival of the Religious Sciences*. Tr. K. Nakamura. Cambridge, 1990.

———. [Book 21] *The Marvels of the Heart*: Kitāb Sharḥ ʿAjā'ib al-Qalb, *Book XXI of the* Iḥyā' ʿUlūm al-Dīn. Tr. Walter james Skellie. Ed. T.J. Winter. Louisville, KY, 2010.

———. [Book 38] *Al-Ghazālī on Vigilance & Self-Examination*: Kitāb al-Murāqaba wa'l-Muḥāsaba, *Book XXXVIII of The Revival of the Religious Sciences*... Tr. Antony F. Shaker. Cambridge, 2015.

———. [Book 39] *Il Libro della Meditazione (Kitāb at-Tafakkur)*. Tr. Giuseppe Celentano. Trieste, 1988.

———[Book 39]. *Le Livre de la Méditation*. Tr. Hassan Boutaleb, Abd-ul-Wadûd Gouraud. Beirut and Paris, 2012.

———. [Book 40] *The Remembrance of Death and the Afterlife:* Kitāb dhikr al-mawt wa mā baʿdahu. *Book XL of The Revival of the Religious*

Sciences… Tr. T.J. Winter. 2nd ed. Cambridge, 2015.

———. *Kīmiyā-yi sa'ādat*, ed. Ḥusayn Khadīw-jam, 2nd ed. 2 vols. Tehran, 1380 sh./2001.

———. [*Kīmiyā-yi sa'ādat*]. *The Alchemy of Happiness*. Tr. Jay R. Crook. 2 vols. Chicago, 2008.

———. *al-Maqṣad al-asnā fī sharḥ ma'ānī Asmā' Allāh al-Ḥusnā*. Ed. Faḍluh Shiḥāda. Beirut, 1971.

———. *The Ninety-Nine Beautiful Names of God*. Tr. David B. Burrell and Nazih Daher. Cambridge, 1999.

Ghazālī, Aḥmad. *Majmū'a-yi āthār-i Fārsī-yi Aḥmad Ghazālī*. Ed. Aḥmad Mujāhid. Tehran, 1376 sh./1997.

al-Ḥaddād, 'Abd Allāh ibn 'Alawī. *Risālat al-Mu'āwana*. 2nd ed. [Beirut], 1414/1994.

———. *The Book of Assistance*. Tr. Mostafa Badawi. London, 1998.

Ibn 'Aṭā' Allāh. *Kitāb al-Ḥikam*. In Aḥmad Zarrūq, *al-Sharḥ al-Ḥādī 'Ashar* (see below).

———. *Ibn 'Aṭā' Allāh (m. 709/1309) et la naissance de la conférie šāḏilite: edition critique et traduction des* Ḥikam. Ed. and tr. Paul Nwyia. Beirut, 1986.

———. *Ibn 'Atā'illāh's Ṣūfī Aphorisms*. Tr. Victor Danner. Leiden, 1973.

Ibn Ḥibbān, Muḥammad. *Kitab al-'Aẓama*. [No edition found].

———. *Ṣaḥīḥ*. Ed. Shu'ayb al-Arnā'ūṭ. Beirut: Mu'assasat al-Risāla, 1993.

Ibn al-Jawzī, 'Abd al-Raḥmān ibn 'Alī. *al-Muntaẓam fī tārīkh al-mulūk wa al-umam*. Riyadh, 2013.

———. *Mukhtaṣar kitab Ṣafwat al-Ṣafwa*. Al-Hufūf, al-Aḥṣā': Maktabat al-Falāh, [1988].

———. *Ṣafwat al-Ṣafwa*. [No edition found].

Ibn al-Qayyim al-Jawziyya, Muḥammad ibn Abī Bakr. *Madārij al-sālikīn*. Ed. 'Abd al-Ḥamīd 'Abd al-Mun'im Madkūr. Cairo, n.d.

———. *Miftāḥ Dār al-sa'āda*. Riyadh: Dār Ibn Khuzayma, 2006.

———. *On Knowledge: from Key to the Blissful Abode*. Tr. Tallal Zeni. Cambridge, 2016.

al-'Irāqī, Zayn al-Dīn 'Abd al-Raḥīm ibn al-Ḥusayn. *al-Jawāhir wa al-durar*. [No edition found]

———. *al-Mughnī 'an al-asfār fī al-asfār fī takhrīj mā fī al-Iḥyā' min al-akhbār*. Cairo, 1993.

al-Kalābādhī, Abū Bakr Muḥammad ibn Isḥāq. *The Doctrine of the Ṣūfīs (Kitāb al-Ta'arruf li-madhhab ahl al-taṣawwuf)*. Tr. A.J. Arberry. Cambridge, 1935.

———. *al-Ta'arruf li-madhhab ahl al-taṣawwuf*. Ed. Aḥmad Shams al-Dīn. Beirut, 1422/2001.

Keeler, Annabel. *Sufi hermeneutics: The Qur'ān commentary of Rashīd al-Dīn Maybudī*. Oxford, 2006.

Khalil, Atif. 'Abū Ṭālib al-Makkī and the Nourishment of Hearts (*Qūt al-qulūb*) in the context of early Sufism.' *The Muslim World*, vol. 122, no. 2 (2012), pp. 1-22.

al-Kharkūshī (= Khargūshī), 'Abd al-Malik ibn Muḥammad. *Tahdhīb al-asrār fī uṣūl al-taṣawwuf*. Ed. Sayyid Muḥammad 'Alī. Beirut, 1427/2006.

Laugier de Beaureceuil, Serge de. *Khwāja 'Abdullāh Anṣārī (396-481 H. 1006-1089), mystique hanbalite*. Beirut, 1965.

Luce, Arthur A. *Teach yourself logic*. London, 1966.

Maḥmūd, Muṣṭafā. *Lughz al-ḥayāh*. Cairo, n.d.

al-Makkī, Abū Ṭālib, *Qūt al-qulūb fī mu'āmalat al-Maḥbūb*. Ed. Sa'īd Nasīb Makārim. Beirut, 2010.

Milne, Joseph. Metaphysics and the Cosmic Order. London, 2008.

Milton, John. *The English Poems of John Milton*. London, 1940.

Muḥammad Mustamlī Bukhārī. *Sharḥ-i Ta'arruf li-madhhab al-taṣawwuf* (sic). Ed. Muḥammad Rawshan. Tehran, 1363 sh./1984.

al-Muḥāsibī, al-Ḥārith *al-Ri'āya li-ḥuqūq Allāh*. Ed. 'Abd al-Qādir Aḥmad 'Aṭā'. Rev. 4th ed. Beirut, n.d.

al-Muḥāsibī, al-Ḥārith ibn Asad. *Kitāb al-Tawahhum*. Ed. A.J. Arberry. Cairo, 1937.

———. *al-Ri'āya li-ḥuqūq Allāh*. Ed. 'Abd al-Qādir Aḥmad 'Aṭā'. Rev. 4th ed. Beirut, n.d.

———. [*Kitāb al-Zuhd*] *al-Masā'il fī a'māl al-qulūb wa al-jawāriḥ, wa ma'ah al-Masā'il fī al-zuhd. Wa Kitāb al-Makāsib, wa Kitāb al-'Aql*. Ed. Khalīl 'Imrān al-Manṣūr. Beirut, 1421/2000.

Muslim ibn al-Ḥajjāj al-Qushayrī. *al-Jāmi' al-Ṣaḥīḥ*. Ed. Muḥammad Fu'ād 'Abd al-Bāqī. Beirut, 1954.

al-Nasā'ī, Aḥmad ibn Shu'ayb. *al-Sunan al-kubrā*. Ed. Markaz al-Buḥūth wa al-Taqniya. Cairo, 2012.

Nasr, Seyyed Hossein. *An Introduction to Islamic Cosmological Doctrines*. Rev. ed. London, 1978.

———. *Islamic Science: an illustrated study*. London, 1976.

Ohlander, Erik S. *Shihāb al-Dīn Suhrawardī and the Rise of the Islamic Mystical Brotherhoods*. Leiden and Boston, 2008.

Picken, Gavin. *Spiritual purification in Islam: the life and works of al-Muḥāsibī*. Abingdon, 2011.

Plato and Xenophon. *Apologies of Socrates*. Ed. Nicholas Denyer. Cambridge, 2019.

Qur'ān.

———. al-Maḥallī, Jalāl al-Dīn and al-Suyūṭī, Jalāl al-Dīn. *Tafsir al-Jalalayn*. [With Arabic text.] Tr. Aisha Bewley. London, 2007.

Ravan Farhadi, A.G. *'Abdullāh Anṣārī of Herat (1006-1089 C.E.): an early Sufi master*. Richmond, UK, 1996.

Rāzī, Najm al-Dīn. *Mirṣād al-'ibād min al-mabda' ilā al-ma'ād*. Ed. Muḥammad Amīn Riyāḥī. Tehran, 1352 sh./1973.

———. *The Path of God's Bondsmen from Origin to Return*. Tr. Hamid Algar. Delmar, NY, 1982.

Renard, John. *Knowledge of God in Classical Sufism: Foundations of Islamic Mystical Theology*. New York and Mahwah, NJ, 2004.

Ritter, Hellmut. *The Ocean of the Soul: Men, the World, and God in the Stories of Farīd al-Dīn 'Aṭṭār*. Tr. J. O'Kane. Leiden and Boston, 2003.

Rūmī, Jalāl al-Dīn Muḥammad. *Fīh mā fīh*. Ed. Badī' al-Zamān Furūzānfar. 2nd ed. Tehran, 1348 sh./1969.

———. *Discourses of Rūmī*. Tr. A.J. Arberry. London, 1961.

———. *Mathnawī, Books I-II, III-IV, V-VI: Text*. Ed. R.A. Nicholson. 3 vols. London, 1925-1933.

———. *Mathnawī, Books I-II, III-IV, V-VI: Translation*. Tr. R.A. Nicholson. 3 vols. London, 1926-1934.

Sanā'ī, Majdūd ibn Ādam. *Sanā'ī-ābād*. In: *Mathnawī-hā-yi Ḥakim Sanā'ī*. Ed. Muḥammad Taqī Raḍawī. Tehran, 1348 sh./1969.

al-Sarrāj, Abū Naṣr. *Kitāb al-Luma' fī al-taṣawwuf*. Ed. R. A. Nicholson. Leiden, 1914.

Shabistarī, Maḥmūd. *Garden of Mystery: the* Gulshan-i rāz *of Mahmud Shabistari*. Tr. Robert Abdul Hayy Darr. Bartlow, UK, 2007.

———. *Gulshan-i rāz*. Ed. Ṣamad Muwaḥḥid. Tehran, 1358 sh./1979.

al-Sharīf al-Raḍī, *Nahj al-balāgha*. Tr. Sayed Ali Reza. New York, 1985.

Smith, Margaret. *An Early Mystic of Baghdad: a study of the life and teaching of al-Ḥārith al-Muḥāsibī, A.D. 781-857*. 2nd ed. London, 1977.

Spiker, Hasan. *Things as they are:* Nafs al-amr *and the ontological foundations of objective truth*. Abu Dhabi, 2017.

Al-Suhrawardī, Shihāb al-Dīn 'Umar. *'Awārif al-ma'ārif*. Ed. Aḥmad 'Abd al-Raḥīm al-Ṣā'iḥ and Tawfīq 'Alī Wahba. Cairo, 1427/2006.

al-Ṭabarānī, Sulaymān ibn Aḥmad. *al-Awsaṭ*. Cairo, 1995.

Thouless, Robert C. *Straight and crooked thinking*. London, 1930.

Tirmidhī, Muḥammad ibn 'Īsā. *al-Jāmi' al-Ṣaḥīḥ*. Ed. Aḥmad Shākir and Muḥammad Fu'ād 'Abd al-Bāqī. Beirut, 1938.

Twerski, Abraham J. *The Spiritual Self: Reflections on Recovery and God*. Center City, MI, 2000.

Waley, Muhammad Isa. 'Contemplative Disciplines in Early Persian Sufism.' In: *Classical Persian Sufism from its Origins to Rumi (700-1300)*, ed. L. Lewisohn (London, 1993), pp. 497-548.

Wiener, Alfred. 'Die *Farağ ba'd al-Šidda* Litteratur', in *Islamica*, 4 (1913).

Wilson, Peter Lamborn, and Pourjavady, Nasrollah. *The Drunken Universe: an anthology of Persian Sufi poetry*. Grand Rapids, MI, 1987.

Wohlleben, Peter. *The Secret Life of Trees: a visual celebration of a magnificent world*. Vancouver, BC; Berkeley, CA, 2018.

———. *The Secret Wisdom of Nature: trees, animals, and the extraordinary balance of all living things: stories from science and observation*. Vancouver, BC; Berkeley, CA, 2019.

Yazaki, Saeko. *Islamic mysticism and Abū Ṭālib al-Makkī*. Hoboken, NJ, 2012.

al-Zabīdī, Murtaḍā. *Itḥāf al-sādat al-muttaqīn*. 10 vols. Cairo, 1311/1893-4.

Zarrūq, Aḥmad. *al-Sharḥ al-Ḥādī 'Ashar 'alā al-Ḥikam al-'Aṭā'iyya*. Ed. Nizār Ḥammādī. Beirut, 1432/2011.

Index of Qurʾānic Verses

Index of Hadiths and Purported Hadiths

Index of Names and Places

Index of Works

Index of Concepts, Terms, and Objects

About the Translator

Muhammad Isa Waley

Muhammad Isa Waley is a British editor, translator and researcher specialising in the literature of Muslim spirituality in Arabic, Persian and Turkish, and also in Islamic manuscript studies. He has an MA in Oriental Studies from the University of Cambridge and a PhD from the School of Oriental and African Studies, London, in Persian literature. For 45 years he was Curator of Persian and Turkish manuscripts and books, first at the British Museum and then at the British Library. He has worked as a consultant and/or editor for many organizations, publishers and individuals, including Al-Furqan Islamic Heritage Foundation, Al Maqasid, Dar al-Taqwa (London), Fawakih, Islamic Art Museum of Malaysia, Islamic Foundation, The Islamic Manuscript Association, *Mawlana Rumi Review*, and Yusuf Islam. Dr Waley's published translations include the *Arbaʿīn* (Forty Hadiths) of Jāmī, *The Book of Remembrances* (Kitāb al-Adhkār) of al-Nawawī, *The Barzanjī Mawlid*, and *Treasury of Rumi*. He has also written catalogues of manuscripts and a number of articles on Sufism and its literature.